# THE

# EVOLUTION OF HINDUSIM

# THE

# EVOLUTION OF HINDUSIM

BY

**MAURICE PHILLIPS**

GYAN

*Published by*

GYAN

Gyan Publishing House
5, Ansari Road
Daryaganj, New Delhi-110002
Phone: 011-47034999, 9811692060
E-mail: books@gyanbooks.com

*Distribution Network*
gyanbooks.com
India, USA, Canada, UK, Australia



ISBN: 978-93-6433-562-1 (HB)
First Published, 1903

2nd Impression 2024

*Printed at:* Gyan Press, Delhi.



**THE EVOLUTION OF HINDUSIM**
Author: MAURICE PHILLIPS

# THE

# EVOLUTION OF HINDUISM

BY

MAURICE PHILLIPS, PH.D.

*Fellow of the University of Madras,*
*Author of "The Teaching of the Vedas, what light does it throw on the Origin and Development of Religion"? "Tumuli in the District of Salem, South India," "A New Upanishad," &c., &c.,*
*Missionary of the London Mission, Madras.*

"Speak of me as I am; nothing extenuate,
Nor set down aught in malice."—*Shakespeare.*

MADRAS:

PRINTED AT THE M. E. PUBLISHING HOUSE, MOUNT ROAD.

1903.

# CONTENTS.

## PART I—The foundation.

## CHAPTER I.

### The Gods of Hinduism.



## CHAPTER II.

### The Goddesses of Hinduism.



## CHAPTER III.

### The Worship of Hinduism.



## CHAPTER IV.

### The Philosophy of Hinduism.

# ERRATA.

| | | | | |
|---|---|---|---|---|
| Pages | 1, 2 | Bráhmanas | *read* | Bráhmaṇas. |
| ,, | 1, 16, 26 | Puránas | ,, | Puráṇas. |
| ,, | 2 | Varuna | ,, | Varuṇa. |
| ,, | 3 | *Kravyad* | ,, | *Kravyád.* |
| ,, | 3 | Vásishta | ,, | Vásishṭa. |
| ,, | 6, 60, 76, 77 | Gauda | ,, | Gauḍa. |
| ,, | 7 | *Prakrits* | ,, | *Prákrits.* |
| ,, | 8 | Niriswara | ,, | Niríswara. |
| ,, | 10, 11, 13 | *bhudhi* | ,, | *bhuddhi.* |
| ,, | 10 | oral | ,, | offal. |
| ,, | 12 | *Drishta* | ,, | *Drishta.* |
| ,, | 13 | *sarira* | ,, | *saríra.* |
| ,, | 13, 23, 24 | *Gunas* | ,, | *Guṇas.* |
| ,, | 14, 20 | Katha | ,, | Kaṭha. |
| ,, | 15 | Krishna | ,, | Krishṇa. |
| ,, | 16, 27 | *Adrista* | ,, | *Adrishta.* |
| ,, | 20 | *evádvitiyam* | ,, | *evádvitíyam.* |
| ,, | 20 | *satiyam* | ,, | *satyam.* |
| ,, | 20 | *mythia* | ,, | *mythya.* |
| ,, | 20 | *jivo* | ,, | *jívo.* |
| ,, | 21 | *advitiya* | ,, | *advitíya.* |
| ,, | 24 | souls | ,, | soul. |
| ,, | 26 | Sudhodana | ,, | Suddhodana. |
| ,, | 26 | Vishnu | ,, | Vishṇu. |
| ,, | 28, 29 | Vedanta | ,, | Vedánta. |
| ,, | 91 | present | ,, | represent. |
| ,, | 109 | paternal | ,, | maternal. |
| ,, | 111 | Aryanr | ,, | Aryans. |

# THE EVOLUTION OF HINDUISM.

## PART I.

### The Foundation.

*Χωρίς γάρ ταύτης, οὔτε τῶν κατὰ λόγον, οὔτε τῶν παρά λόγον εἶναι δοκούντων οὐδέν οἷόν τε συντεγεσθῆναι.*—
*Polybius.*

Hinduism denotes the various religious beliefs and practices now prevalent in India. It differs from Vedism*, or Bráhmanism, in being more vague and comprehensive. Vedism, or Bráhmanism, denotes the ancient religion of the Hindu-Aryans, as contained in the Vedas and Bráhmanas, in contradistinction to the religions of the aboriginal inhabitants. Hinduism comprises the religions of to-day, which are neither Vedic nor aboriginal, but a fusion of corrupt Vedic doctrines with aboriginal non-Aryan cults. Its literature is not the Veda, but the epic poems, the Rámáyana and Mahábhárata, and the more recent Puránas.

How came the Vedic doctrines to be corrupted? What made this fusion possible? Or, what were the factors which conditioned Hinduism? is our enquiry in this Part.

We may not be able to discover all the subtle factors which made Hinduism possible and necessary, but there can be no doubt that the chief are—(i) The disintegration of Vedism, and (ii) The reaction of the Bráhmans.

---

* For an account of Vedism see "The Teaching of the Vedas," by Maurice Phillips. Longmans & Co., 1895; and Addison & Co., Madras.

# CHAPTER I.

## The Disintegration of Vedism.

The disintegration of Vedism was caused by—(1) The invariable tendency of human nature to corrupt religion; (2) The commingling of the Aryans with the Aborigines; (3) The cultivation of Philosophy; and (4) The rise of Buddhism.

1.—*The invariable tendency of human nature to corrupt religion.*

The science of "Comparative Religion" has proved beyond a doubt that this tendency was at work among the Aryans before they left the primeval home. And it is clearly seen in the Vedas, the Bráhmanas and the Upanishads. "If there is one thing," says the late Professor Max Müller, "which a comparative study of religions places in the clearest light, it is the inevitable decay to which every religion is exposed. . . Whenever we trace back a religion to its first beginnings, we find it free from many blemishes that offend us in its later phases."*

In "The Teaching of the Vedas: what light does it throw on the Origin and Development of Religion?" the author has furnished ample evidence to show that in proportion as we push our enquiries up to the source of the Vedic religion, the simpler and purer we find it; and that in proportion as we come down the stream, the more complex and turbid it appears. In the most ancient hymns addressed to Varuna, the oldest god of the Vedas, the conception of the Supreme Being is far more sublime and God-like, and the ethical consciousness of sin far

* "Chips from a German workshop." Vol. I. Preface, pp. xxiii. iv.

more vivid and intense, than they are in subsequent hymns addressed to later deities.

This tendency in the religious sphere is similar to that which Evolutionists call "arrested development" in the natural world. Both are states in which "continuous progress" is checked, and deterioration, more or less continuous, is introduced. This tendency is co-extensive with man, and hence its effects are everywhere visible in the religious history of mankind.

2.—*The commingling of the Aryans with the Aborigines.*

When the Aryans, who are now represented chiefly by the Bráhmans and the Rájputs, crossed the Indus about 1500 B.C., they encountered a strange, uncouth people, who differed greatly from themselves in colour, in language, in religion and in custom. These, in consequence of the opposition which they offered to the advance of their conquerors, are described in the Vedas in most odious terms as *dasyus*, enemies; *dâsa*, slaves; *râkshasas*, barbarians; *kravyad*, raw flesh eaters; *avritas*, devoid of religious rites; *abrahma*, priestless; *anagnitra*, not keeping the sacred fire; *achitas*, mad; *mûradevas*, worshippers of mad gods; *krishnayonis*, people of black colour.* They were even accused of eating human flesh! Thus we read, "The Yátudhánas who gloat on the bloody flesh of men and horses, and steal the milk of the cow! O Agni, cut off their heads with thy fiery sword."† There is no reason, however, to believe that this description of the aborigines by their conquering enemies is strictly correct, for we find that their great Rishi Vásishta, when in feud with the Rája-rishi Visvá-

* Phillips' Teaching of the Vedas, p. 178.

† R. V., X. 87. 2.

mitra, is called not only an enemy, but a Yátudhána or demon! Some of them were doubtless in a savage or semi-savage state, but probably the majority were fairly civilized, for they lived in fortified cities, fought with weapons, possessed much wealth and were governed by kings.*

The Aryans in the course of centuries subjugated the aboriginal inhabitants of the north from the Indus to the Ganges, and from the Himálayas to the Vindhya mountains, and both Aryans and aborigines gradually coalesced into one community; of which the former composed the upper, and the latter the lower, classes. Afterwards the Aryans turned their faces to the south, under the leadership of Ráma, and attempted to conquer the indigenous races. They crossed the Vindhya mountains, but tried in vain to subdue the people by force of arms as they had done those of the north, hence they failed to impose their language upon them; the languages of the south remaining to this day Turanian and little influenced by Sanskrit. They conquered the inhabitants of the south, however, by the more honourable weapons of learning and higher civilization. Bráhman missionaries, the most distinguished of whom was Agastya, dwelt among them, learnt their languages, and gradually so insinuated themselves into the good graces of the people as to be able to impose their institutions upon them. When Ráma came to the south, the Rishis represented the inhabitants to him in these words: "Men-devouring Râkshasas of various shapes, and wild beasts, which feed on blood, dwell in this vast forest. They harass the devotees, who reside in the settlements, and slay them. These shapeless and ill-looking monsters testify their abominable character by various cruel and terrific displays.

* Muir's Sanskrit Texts, Part II, pp. 334-405.

These base-born wretches implicate the hermits in impure practices and perpetrate the greatest outrages. Changing their shapes, and hiding in the thickets adjoining the hermitages, these frightful beings delight in terrifying the devotees. They cast away the sacrificial ladles and vessels. They pollute the cooked oblations, and utterly defile the offerings with blood. These faithless creatures inject frightful sounds into the ears of the faithful and austere eremites. At the time of sacrifice, they snatch away the jars, the flowers, the fuel, and the sacred grass, of these sober-minded men."*

---

* रक्षांसि पुरुषादीनि नानारूपाणि राघव ।
वसन्त्यस्मिन् महारण्ये व्यालाश्च रुधिराशनाः ॥

उत्साद्य तापसान् सर्वान् जनस्थाननिवासिनः ।
घ्नन्ति चास्मिन् महारण्ये तान् निवारय राघव ॥

दर्शयन्त्यतिबीभत्सं क्रूरैर्भीषणकैरपि ।
नानारूपैर्विरूपास्ते रूक्षैरशुभदर्शनाः ॥

उपचारैरशुचिभिः संप्रयुज्य च तापसान् ।
दर्शयन्ति परां हिंसामनार्य्याः पुरुषर्षभ ॥

गहनेष्वाश्रमान्तेषु लीना विकृतदर्शनाः ।
रमन्ते तापसांस्तत्र त्रासयन्तः सुदारुणाः ॥

अपक्षिपन्ति स्रुग्भाण्डं दूषयन्ति शृतं हविः ।
शोणितैर्बलिकर्माणि नाशयन्ति समन्ततः ॥

विश्वस्तानां अविश्वस्तास्तापसानां तपस्विनाम् ।
भैरवं कर्णमूलेषु विसृजन्ति महास्वनम् ॥

Rámáyana III. X. 6; II. 116, 14-17.

This description is evidently exaggerated; for it is stated in another place in the Rámáyana that the sage Agastya was able to restrain them by kindness, and to render the southern regions perfectly secure. "Ever since," we read, "the holy man has resided in this region, all the goblins have become subject to him. Through the name of this saint the southern country has become prosperous, and renowned in the three worlds. No liar, or cruel, fiendish, impure, oppressive or wretched man may dwell there."*

Ethnologically the aboriginal races of India are Turanian in contradistinction to Aryan. Dr. Oppert calls them Gauda-Dravidian, Gauda denoting the northern and Dravidian the southern aborigines. Philologically they are divided into Tibeto-Burman, Kolarian and Dravidian. All came to India in pre-historic times after living somewhere in Central Asia side by side with the ancestors of the Mongols and the Chinese. The first and second are supposed to have entered India through the north-east pass, and the third, who inhabit the south, through the north-west, the pass through which the Aryans afterwards came.

The religion of the Aryans is Physiolatry, or the worship of the elements and activities of nature. The

---

* यदाप्रभृति चाक्रान्ता दिगियं पुण्यकर्मणा ।
तदाप्रभृति सर्वेऽस्य प्रशान्ता रजनीचराः ॥
नाम्ना चेयं भगवतो दक्षिणा दिक् प्रदक्षिणा ।
प्रथिता त्रिषु लोकेषु दुष्प्रेक्ष्या क्रूरकर्मभिः ॥
नात्र जीवेद् मृषावादी क्रूरो नैकृतिकोऽशुचिः ॥
नृशंसः पापवृत्तो वा अनिष्णो यस्तथाविधः ॥

Rámáyana III. XI. 83, 84.

religion of the aborigines is Fetichism and Animalism. The former adore the heaven and the earth, the sun, the fire, the wind, the storm, the dawn, the mountains and the rivers. These deities comprise matter and spirit, the elements and the invisible powers behind them.* The latter worship stones, trees, serpents, monkeys, vultures, fish and other animals.

Now, it is well known that Sanskrit, the language of the ancient Aryans, deteriorated under the operation of the general laws to which all languages are subject, and by contact with the languages of the aboriginal tribes, resulting in the formation of the *prakrits*, the vernaculars now spoken in north and west India. In like manner Vedism, the ancient religion of the Aryans, deteriorated, partly in consequence of the invariable tendency of human nature to corrupt religion, and partly in consequence of contact with the religions of the aborigines, culminating in the disintegration of the ancient creed and making the Evolution of Hinduism possible.

3.—*The Cultivation of Philosophy.*

The Hindus have not been inaptly called a "nation of philosophers." It is in philosophy and in grammar that they have attained their highest distinction. In the former they are equal, and in the latter they are superior, to the Greek masters.

The study of philosophy began in India at a very early period. There are a few hymns both in the Atharva and the Rig Vedas of a deeply speculative character, which indicate a long period of profound reflection on the origin and nature of things. The Upanishads, the last portions of the Vedas, are little more than curious metaphysical dis-

* Phillips' Teaching of the Vedas, pp. 29-112.

quisitions on God, Man, and the Universe. Between them and the formulated systems of philosophy there is probably a literary gap of two or three hundred years. But the superiority of the systems over the Upanishads shows clearly that, meanwhile, the study of philosophy had been constantly and energetically pursued.

The Hindus have six systems of *orthodox* philosophy, *viz.*, the Nyáya, founded by Gautama; the Vaiseshika, by Kanáda; the Sánkhya, by Kapila; the Yoga, by Patanjali; the Mímánsá, by Jaimini; and the Vedánta, by Bádaráyana or Vyása; and three systems of *heterodox* philosophy, *viz.*, Buddhism, Jainism, and Chárvákism. Buddhism we shall consider later on, Jainism is akin to it, and Chárvákism is a system of gross materialism.

The Vaiseshika being in a way supplementary to the Nyáya, the two are grouped together under the name Nyáya; and as the case is similar with the Yoga and Sánkhya, and with the Mímánsá and Vedánta, it is customary to speak of Hindu Philosophy as being divicible into the Nyáya, the Sánkhya, and the Vedánta. The Nyáya and Vaiseshika are alike in doctrine; the former being occupied chiefly with the principles of investigating truth, and the latter with the objects to be investigated. The Sánkhya in its structures and tenets is closely followed by the Yoga. The great difference between the two is that the former is *Níriswara, Sine Deo*, the latter *Samíswara, Cum Deo.* The Mímánsá, called also Púrva Mímánsá, expounds the earlier portions of the Vedas, and describes the ceremonial observances by which religious merit may be acquired. Like the Sánkhya it ignores God; but unlike the Sánkhya, it magnifies the Veda above all things, declaring that it exists eternally without any dependence on an eternal Authorizer, or Revealer. This it supports by asserting the eternity of sound, or that an eternal sound underlies all temporary sounds, which sound is the Veda. The Vedánta, called also Uttara Mímánsá, expounds the Upanishads, and develops the higher mode of meditation on the nature and attributes of the supreme Brahma by which absorption into his essence may be more speedily and effectually attained.

The great object of the three systems is eminently religious, for it is the liberation of the soul from misery. Sin as the violation of divine law is not recognised, but misery as the result of the union of the soul with matter, real or fictitious, is the great burden of the three. That union produces ignorance (*avidyà*), which consists in the soul identifying itself with the mind, the senses and the body, while in reality it is altogether distinct from them. In consequence of this identification, the soul imagines that some things are its own and some things belong to others; hence arise desire and aversion:—desire for what it thinks gives pleasure, and aversion to what it thinks gives pain. By reason of desire and aversion the soul engages in various works, good and evil, from which accrue merit and demerit; the fruits of both it must reap in heaven, in hell and in repeated births. Liberation, therefore, according to the Sánkhya and Nyáya, is the right apprehension on the part of the soul that it is an entity apart from the mind, the senses and the body; and according to the Vedánta that it is nothing but a portion of the all, or Brahma. *

* Some Vedantists say that the soul is a portion of Brahma appropriated to the internal organ, and others that it is a reflexion of Brahma in the internal organ.

The fundamental principles of the Sánkhya are "Nature" (*prakriti*) and "Soul" (*âtman*). *Prakriti* is an eternally self-existent, subtile, invisible essence, composed of goodness, (*sattva*) passion, (*rajas*) and darkness (*tamas*) in three equal parts, the existence of which is inferred from its effects. Soul is individual, multitudinous, eternal and immortal. Soul existing alone with Nature and being attracted to it, like the needle to the loadstone, is united to Nature for the purpose of contemplating it, and ultimately of being liberated from its influence. Neither can do anything by itself; hence both join together, just as the lame and the blind join together for mutual guidance and locomotion in a journey. By that union creation is effected, but the soul does not seem to do anything, for all creation, we are told, proceeds from Nature (*prakriti*) as spontaneously as cream from milk. Nature, therefore, is both the substantial and the efficient cause of the universe; God being altogether ignored.

Starting from *prakriti*, which means that which 'evolves or produces,' the Sánkhya proceeds to construct the world by evolution. From *prakriti*, we are told, proceeds *budhi*, intellect; from *budhi*, *ahankára*, self-consciousness, or egoism; from *ahankára* the five subtile rudiments of the objects of sense—odour, tangibleness, sapidity, visibility and sound,—from which are educed the five gross elements, earth, air, water, fire and ether. From *ahankára* also proceed the five organs of sense, eye, nose, tongue, ear, and skin; and the five organs of action, the voice, the hands, the feet, the oral orifice and the organ of generation, as well as *manas*, mind, which is an internal organ, and is the eleventh. *Ahankára* and *manas* are not attributes of the soul, but of *prakriti*, unintelligent matter. These eleven organs and the two principles,—*budhi*, intellect, and *ahankára*, egoism, are the thirteen instruments of knowledge; ten external and three internal.

The distinguishing function of *budhi*, intellect, is certitude; of *ahankára*, egoism, the cognition of the self as the one affected in sensation; and of *manas*, mind, discrimination, or the admittance of only separate sensations to the intellect. "An external sense perceives; the internal *manas* examines, or discriminates; egoism makes the selfish application; and intellect resolves what it is and exhibits it to the soul." 'Therefore the apprehension or cognition of some external object such as—'this is a jar, or this is cloth'—is not a direct action of the soul but an emanation from the internal organ which consists of intellect, egoism, and mind.' This organ, it is affirmed, assumes the form of a jar, of cloth, &c., and this assumption is called an affection. Thus the cognition, this is a jar, or this is a cloth, is an affection of the internal organ; but in consequence of the proximity to each other of the internal organ and the soul, each is reflected in the other. Hence the affection of the internal organ in the shape of a jar or cloth is reflected in the soul. Consequently the reflection in the soul of the affection-apprehension is the soul's apprehension. Similarly, will and activity are reflections of the internal organ, and the soul by reason of receiving their reflections, imagines itself a willer and a doer; consequently it has to experience happiness, misery, heaven, hell and rebirths as the real fruit of imaginary good and evil deeds. For the soul, though not actually a doer, but falsely thinking itself one, is brought into the bondage of experiencing the fruit of works; and this is the bondage of the soul.

Eternal *Prakriti* and its twenty-three productions, together with Soul (*purusha*), are the twenty-five principles, or categories, of the Sánkhya philosophy, and hence its name Sánkhya "enumeration." A correct knowledge of these categories on the part of the soul will result in beatitude which is a state resembling that of deep sleep.* The Yoga adds a supreme Soul, or God, to the categories of the Sánkhya, and declares that intense devotion to Him by means of penance and mortification of the flesh will secure the same desired end.

The means by which a correct knowledge of the principles, or categories, of the Sánkhya, may be acquired are three, *viz.*, *Drishta*, *Anumána*, and *Apta vacána*, perception by the senses, inference, and credible assertion, or trustworthy testimony. Intuition is the only other mode of legitimate knowledge, but it is confined to superior beings. Perception is regarded as the first kind of evidence. Inference is of three kinds :—(1) Inference of an effect from seeing its cause in operation; "It will rain, because clouds are gathering." (2) Inference of a cause from observing its effects; "There is a fire on the hill, for I see smoke." (3) Inference from a relation different from both, as when the colour of a flower is inferred from its scent, and the saltness of the sea from that of some of its waters. Testimony, or tradition, denotes both the Vedas, which are believed to have emanated from Brahma, and the recollections of those who remember events in their former births.

---

समाधि सुषुप्ति मोक्षेषु ब्रह्मरूपता=

* Sánkhya-Pravachana-bháshya, p. 204, as quoted by N. N. S. Gore in Rational Refutation of the Hindu Philosophical Systems, p. 33.

In relation to causality, the Sánkhya principles are thus described:—Nature, (*prakriti*) root all, is no product. Seven principles, *budhi*, *ahankára* and the five subtile elements are products and producers. The remaining sixteen are products. Causes and effects are essentially the same; there is no difference between a product and that which produces it. The soul alone is neither a product nor a producer.

The soul is invested with a subtile body, about the size of a thumb, and is called *linga sarira*, or *súkshma sarîra.* It is the first creation, produced at the very earliest development of activities from the original *prakriti.* It is unconfined, too subtile for restraint, swift as the wind, and cannot enjoy till it is united to a grosser body (*sthûla sarîra*). This subtile body is the abode of the soul till it attains final emancipation. It travels with it through all its migrations in the three worlds.

The three *gunas* or qualities, goodness (*sattva*), passion, (*raja*), and darkness, (*tamas*) which enter into the composition of primeval Nature in three equal parts, and by which ancient philosophers tried to account for the presence of good and evil in the world, necessarily enter into everything evolved from Nature (*prakriti*) but not in equal parts. In the original producer they are equal, but in the produced they vary, one or other being in excess. 'A preponderance of goodness in man makes him divine and noble, a preponderance of passion human and selfish, a preponderance of darkness ignorant and bestial. These *gunas* are the triple-cord, by which the soul, like an animal, is bound.'

Kapila's theory of the origin of the universe and especially his representation of intellect, self-consciousness and mind, as natural substances and not as qualities of the soul, are curious in the extreme. How are such notions to be accounted for? They seem to have existed before Kapila. We read in the Katha Upanishad,* "Beyond the senses there are the objects; beyond the objects there is the mind (*manas*); beyond the mind there is the intellect (*buddhi*); beyond the intellect there is the great self; beyond the great one, there is the highest undeveloped (*avyakta*); beyond the undeveloped there is the person (*purusha*) the all-presiding, characterless. Whosoever knows him is liberated and obtains immortality." Here we have mind, intellect, the great self, which may be the same as Kapila's self-consciousness, and the highest undeveloped (*avyakta*), which according to the Bhagavad-Gíta is *prakriti*. Kapila, therefore, might have conceived the idea of his system by contemplating this passage. But to say this is only to throw back the difficulty a step further. What we want to know is 'how did such an idea originate?' There are two explanations:—"Tracing back the soul's most active life in the body, in the day-time as contrasted with night, in manhood as contrasted with infancy, the idea that until united with body in some form, the soul's powers lie in a dormant state might have originated it. These powers are not exerted until an adequate occasion calls them forth. But when soul is united to matter (*prakriti*), intelligence, the first dawning of mental life and power, begins to appear. Mistaking occasion for cause, one might think this intelligence to be the product of "Nature," instead of the product of soul occasioned by the union between the two; and as intelligence continues to act, there springs up within the sphere

* I. 3, 11, 6, 7.

of its activity the thought of self. Further on, in the sphere of self-consciousness, are produced the germs of subtile particles (notions) of the five elements; notions of the organs of which the body is constructed; and further on, as Berkeley thought, the notions of an external world." This is Dr. Mullen's explanation.* Mr. N. N. Sastri Gore offers the following:—'It is written in the Veda, with reference to God, that at the time the world was made, 'He saw' and said 'I am one.' 'I would become many.' By these words perception and self-consciousness are implied to have arisen in God at the beginning of the Universe. Perception is intellect and the notion denoted by 'I' is egoism. From this the ancients might have concluded, that God, in order to create the world, assumed intellect and egoism as the causes of the world. And having long been used to consider His intellect and egoism as the instrumental causes of the world, gradually came to look upon them as independent objects and ultimately as the material causes of the world.' †

The Sánkhya appears to be the oldest of the formulated systems of Hindu Philosophy. Buddhism has much in common with it, and its ideas are prevalent in the Mahábhárata. In that book Krishna is described as an undeveloped *prakriti*, and Siva as the cause of the causes of the world and therefore superior and antecedent to *pradhána*, (another name for *prakriti*) and *purusha*. It is also stated, "There is no knowledge equal to the Sánkhya and no power equal to the Yoga." The Bhagavad-Gíta is an eclectic system of philosophy based on the principles of the Sánkhya

* Religious Aspect of Hindu Philosophy, pp. 54-5.

† N. N. Sastri Gore's Rational Refutation of the Hindu Philosophical Systems, p. 83.

and the asceticism of the Yoga. Nearly half the Purânas follow the cosmology of the Sánkhya. Professor Weber says: "The most flourishing epoch of the Sánkhya-Yoga belongs most probably to the first century of our era; the influence it exercised upon the development of gnosticism in Asia Minor being unmistakable; while further, both through this channel and afterwards directly, it had an important influence upon the growth of Sufi-Philosophy."*

The Nyáya, which means propriety or fitness, postulates an *Isvara*, God, Soul, and eternally pre-existing Atoms, as its fundamental principles. From these atoms *Isvara* either formed the world, or it proceeded spontaneously by the power of *Adrishta*, the *Unseen*, under his superintendence. An atom, we are told, is the minutest portion of visible objects, and incapable of further division. From the aggregation of atoms the Universe was formed. Atoms have neither a beginning nor an end; but their aggregates, the elements—earth, water, fire, air and ether—have a beginning, and are liable to destruction. Time, space, mind and soul are also eternal and everlasting.

The supreme Soul, or God, is described as one, eternal, omnipotent, without form, pervading everything, framer of the world, and bestower of the consequences of the good and evil actions of inferior souls. Souls are eternal, immortal, all-pervading, and yet distinct from bodies, senses and mind. To souls belong apprehension, will, activity, happiness, misery, virtue and vice; but only so much of the soul as dwells in the body can see, hear, apprehend, will and enjoy. All the wretchedness of the soul arises from imagining that it is identical with the body; and emancipation consists in a right knowledge of itself.

* Sanskrit Literature, p. 239. Trubner's Oriental Series.

The objects of knowledge, according to Gautama, are—soul, body, senses, objects of sense, understanding or intellection, mind, activity, faults, temptation, fruits or consequences, pain and beatitude. Kanáda in the Vaiseshika is more philosophical and reduces these to six, *viz.*, substance, quality, action, genus, difference and intimate relation. Mind and soul are among the substances.

Like the Sánkhya, the Nyáya represents the soul and mind as altogether different entities. The soul is all-pervading; the mind is in the form of an eternal atom. The soul is the self, and the mind is the organ, which, standing between the soul and the deliverances of sense, prevents those deliverances from crowding in *pell mell;* just as the minister stands between the monarch and the thousand simultaneous claims upon his attention, and hands up for his consideration one thing at a time. The soul is known by knowledge, volition, desire, aversion, pleasure and pain; and the mind by the non-arising of cognitions in the soul simultaneously. Grant that our cognitions are consecutive and not simultaneous; to account for this, Dugald Stewart says that the mind can attend to only one thought at a time. Gautama, recognizing the same fact, but speaking of the knower invariably as soul, accounts for it by assuming that there is an instrument, *manas*, mind, through which alone knowledge can reach the soul, and which, as it gives admission to only one thought at a time, is inferred to be no larger than an atom. Such an atomic inlet to the soul may be illustrated by the organ of vision; for though the whole body is presented to the rays reflected from external objects, it is only through a special channel, the *eye,* that these find entrance so as to cause knowledge. The soul, then, may be practically regarded as corresponding to the thinking principle, and the mind to the faculty of attending to one, and only one thing at a time. It must be remembered, however, that according to the Nyáya the mind is not a faculty, but a substance.

The next object of knowledge after mind is activity, described as that which originates the utterances of the voice, the notions of the understanding and the gestures of the body; all intended to secure the rewards of virtue and vice and to keep up the condition of illusion in which men live. This activity is caused by our faults, and appears in the three forms of *affection*, *aversion*, and *infatuation*. Pain is defined as that which is characterized by uneasiness, and absolute deliverance therefrom is beatitude.

The instruments of knowledge are four, *viz.*, perception (*Pratyaksha*), inference (*Anumána*), comparison (*Upamána*) and testimony (*Sabda*). With these instruments all the objects of knowledge must be examined with the view of arriving at right conclusions respecting them.

The demonstration of every conclusion contains five elements, *viz.*, the proposition, which states what is to be established; the reason by means of which its establishment is secured; the example which furnishes some familiar feature of the fact; the application of the example to that which is to be established; and the conclusion in which the original proposition is declared to be proved. These five elements form the Nyáya Syllogism which is thus illustrated :—

| | | |
|---|---|---|
| Proposition | ... | The hill is fiery. |
| Reason | ... | For it smokes. |
| Example | ... | Whatever smokes is fiery. |
| Application | ... | The hill is smoking. |
| Conclusion | ... | The hill is fiery. |

When by these instruments and processes correct knowledge of existing things is acquired, false notions depart; on their departure, the fault of concerning oneself about external objects ceases; on its cessation there is nothing to call for either reward or punishment, for either pain, or rebirth; and the absence of these is the Nyáya conception of the *summum bonum.*

'Of all the Hindu philosophical systems the Nyáya-Vaiseshika is the best and nearest in its methods to those of European systems. In spite of its imperfect analysis and generalizations, it has found a great deal of solid truth. In its method of enquiry, and in the laws which it prescribed to the instruments of investigation, it reached the method which modern science employs. It allows a substantial existence to the Universe, while the Sánkhya allows only an ideal existence of aggregate qualities; and the Vedánta an illusive existence, the effect of *Máyá.* Both the Sánkhya and the Nyáya classify causes into material and instrumental, and postulate the law that "from nothing nothing comes." The Sánkhya asserts the identity of cause and effect, holding that effects are only the same as their causes; while the Nyáya allows the fact, so often shown in modern chemistry, that the operation of two causes may result in a third kind of product different in form and quality from both, though actually produced by their mutual action.'

The superiority of the Nyáya in its analysis of spirit and matter, as compared with the Sánkhya, seems to indicate its lateness in time. The Sánkhya, though atheistic, moves within the circle of Vedic ideas; whereas the Nyáya breathing more freely, relies more upon the powers of reason, and reminds us of the circle of thoughts in which Aristotle moved.

The Vedánta, as its name implies, is the end of the Veda, or the doctrines scattered in the Upanishads formulated into a system. The teaching of the Sánkhya and the Nyáya is subversive of the Monism, or Pantheism, of the Upanishads, and hence the necessity of defending it. This the Vedánta undertook; consequently, as a *system* it is posterior to the Sánkhya and Nyáya, though its subject matter is prior to both. Indeed the germs of the Vedánta are found in the *Purusha Sûkta* of the Rig-Veda, and its fundamental principle is distinctly enunciated in the Katha-Upanishad, *ekam evádvitiyam*, 'one essence without a second'*; and that essence is Brahma. *Brahma sattyam, jagan mithiâ, jivo brahmaiva nâparah*,† 'Brahma is true, the world is false, the soul is only Brahma and no other.' In the second Aphorism of Vyása, Brahma is described as "that from which the production of the Universe results." The Universe, therefore, is an emanation from Brahma and even that emanation is not real but illusory. Brahma in his essence is "spirit," "existence," "knowledge," "joy"; devoid of qualities and acts; in whom there is no consciousness such as is denoted by "I," "thou" and "it"; who apprehends no person, nor thing, nor is apprehended of any; who is neither omniscient nor omnipresent; who has neither beginning nor end; who is immutable and indefectible and the only true entity.‡ All else is false or nothing

* Chap. VI. 2.

† ब्रह्मसत्यं जगत् मिथ्या जीवो ब्रह्मैव नाऽपरः ॥

‡ निष्कलं निष्क्रियं शान्तं निरवद्यं निरञ्जनं ॥
S'wetas'watara Upanishad, Bibliotheca Indica, Vol. VII. p. 370.

whatever. "All this Universe indeed is Brahma; from him does it proceed; into him it is dissolved; in him it breathes."* There is no difference between Brahma, the supreme Soul, and the individual soul, as there is none between the sky which covers the trees and the forests and the sky which is reflected in the ocean and in many waters. The individual soul is a portion of Brahma appropriated to the internal organ. Hence the internal organ—consisting of intellect, egoism and mind—is represented in the Vedánta, as it is in the Sánkhya, as possessing characteristics which belong only to the soul! This being the Vedánta doctrine of true existence, it is denominated *advitiya*, non-dual or monistic.

The stubborn actuality of external things, however, compelled the Vedántists to postulate a second kind of existence applicable to such, and the character they gave to that existence compelled them to add a third. These three existences are—Real, Practical and Apparent.† Real existence is Brahma, Practical existence is predicable of *Isvara*, the world and all things therein. These do not really exist; the ignorant mistake them for existent, and use them as the means of transacting the practical duties of life. And as these

---

* Chand. U. III. 14.

† त्रिविधं सत्वं पारमार्थिकं व्यावहारिकं प्रातिभासिकं चेति । तत्र पारमार्थिकं सत्त्वं ब्रह्मणः व्यावहारिकं सत्त्वमाकाशादेः प्रातिभासिकं सत्त्वं शुक्तिरजतादेः ॥

Vedánta Paribhásha, p. 18, Gore's Rational Refutation of the Hindu Philosophical Systems, p. 156.

themselves are only imaginary, so is their use. For example, a man in a dream drinks water or mounts a horse, and as the water and the horse are visionary and devoid of all reality, so are the drinking and the mounting. Apparent existence resembles the practical in being false, but differs from it in three things: (1) The ignorant do not constantly, but only occasionally, mistake what is true for apparent objects, as nacrine for silver and the matter of a dream. (2) There is no practical dealing with these objects. Let a man who mistakes nacrine for silver offer it for sale, and he will not get the price of silver for it. (3) It is because of ignorance that the practical seems true, but in addition to this, and other causes called defects, the apparent seems true. From the practical existence point of view there is an *Isvara*, God, the maker of the world, who is all-wise and all-powerful; there are souls, their ignorance, their doing good and evil, their requital in heaven and hell, and their transmigration and final beatitude. But from the Real existence point of view all these are absolutely non-existent. "Neither are they, nor have they been, nor are they to be! Brahma alone exists, all beside is illusory, owing its existence to the imagination of ignorance, just as the terrible snake that is imagined in the rope neither has been, nor is, nor will be.

But how, it may be asked, can a world, the very essence of falsehood, be the manifestation of a true existence? The answer is—"The world is false only because of the ignorance (*avidyà*) which regards it as true. Brahma, ignoring himself by a sort of self-imposed ignorance, drew out from himself for his own amusement, all souls and all appearances, which though really parts of his essence, constitute the phenomena of the Universe." This ignorance is, like the Sánkhya *prakriti*, an aggregate of the three *gunas* or qualities, and in respect to individual souls, it has two powers, *viz.*, a *covering* and a *producing.** The covering power hides the infinite soul and makes it limited; the producing power gives rise to notions of happiness, misery, possession and dominion; and as it educes an unreal snake from a real rope, so in the soul it produces the expanses of the Universe, and projects them as phantoms before the mind's eye. Nevertheless, the soul which is covered by it is one soul. When the individual soul, by means of the Vedánta philosophy, gets rid of this ignorance, it will perceive that the world is not false, it is all Brahma!

There is a close resemblance between the Vedánta and the systems of Kapila and Gautama. The world according to Kapila, was spontaneously evolved from eternally self-existent subtile Nature in conjunction with Soul without an *Isvara*, or *Demiurgos*; and according to Gautama, it was formed under the superintendence of *Isvara* from eternally pre-existent atoms. The Vedánta represents the world as having been made by *Isvara* from eternal ignorance, (*avidyà*) and the order of creation is nearly the same as that of the Sánkhya, whilst it recognises most of the

---

* अस्याऽज्ञानस्याऽऽवरणविक्षेपनामकं शक्तिद्वयमस्ति। आवरणशक्तिरित्यावत् * * * * * अज्ञान परिच्छिन्नमप्याऽऽत्मानमपरिच्छिन्नमसंसारिणमवलोकयितृबुद्धिपिधायकतयाऽऽच्छादयतीव तादृशं सामर्थ्यम् ॥

Vedánta Sára, pp. 6, 7. Gore's Rational Refutation of the Hindu Philosophical Systems, p. 248.

objects of knowledge mentioned by the Nyáya. The soul being incapable of cognition without the aid of the mind, is common to all three. The mind is held by the Sánkhya and Vedánta to stand between the organs of perception and those of action, partaking of the nature of each. But while the Sánkhya divides the internal organ into intellectual perception, self-consciousness and the reasoning mind,—the first being the great source of the others,—the Vedánta adds a fourth, *chitta*, the faculty of thought. It also adds two instruments of knowledge, non-perception or negative proof, and inference from circumstances, to the four admitted by the Nyáya; while the Sánkhya rejects the Nyaya's comparison and retains as its only three instruments, perception by the senses, inference and testimony.

The Vedánta agrees with the Sánkhya that every soul is invested with a subtile as well as with a gross body, and that every portion of the Universe is invested with the three *gunas*. The three systems affirm that what has no beginning will have no end.

It must not be forgotten, however, that the resemblance between the Vedánta and the other two is only a resemblance from the standpoint of *Practical* existence. From the standpoint of *Real* existence there is none; for there is neither *Isvara*, souls, nor Universe, all are the imagination of ignorance. Brahma alone exists; and as he is void of qualities he is the substrate of no predicates, and hence philosophically is nothing. The philosophy of the Vedánta, therefore, is a philosophy of Nihilism; its pure existence, entity or being, is identical with pure nothing! And strange to say, it always has been, and is to-day, the most popular philosophy in India!

Dr. Mullens, in his "Religious Aspects of Hindu

Philosophy,"* says, "The moral feelings are entirely omitted from all the systems. None of them enter into our notions of justice, compassion, veracity, love and gratitude. They say nothing of the domestic affections, nor of anger and jealousy, the defensive affections by which our interests are protected. Conscience is never referred to as a ruling moral power, probably from the reason, that good and evil are ascribed to the Supreme rather than to the fault and folly of men. Nor are the various classes of moral duties among men as members of society or of a family, or as men in general, discussed. All feelings and desires are by the various systems reckoned imperfections."

All these systems of philosophy seem to have gradually grown up together in different schools. They pre-suppose each other and argue with each other; the doctrines having been retouched and interpolated in later times, all seem to have sprung into existence on the same day. "The Sutras, as we have them, cannot be the original forms of the doctrines of the several schools; they are rather a recapitulation of a series of preceding developments which had gone on in the works of successive teachers."† It is impossible to fix the age of any of them. That they are post Vedic, we know, for they acknowledge the Vedas as possessing supreme authority, though the Nyáya and Sánkhya are often at variance with them. They are written in Sutras, and so belong to what is called the "Sutra Period," which is supposed to range between 600 and 200 B. C. Recent researches, however, make it necessary to extend the latter limit

---

* Page 171. † Cowell's note in Colebrook's Essays.

considerably, for it is found that the Sánkhya Sutras, as we have them, are as late as the 14th Century A. D.

The authors to whom the systems are attributed are probably mythical. Bádaráyana, or Veda-vyása, the reputed author of the Vedánta, is said to have been the arranger of the Veda, (whence his name Veda-vyása) and the author of the Mahábhárata. This, however, is impossible, for the collection of the Vedic hymns, the composition of the Mahábhárata and the formation of the Vedánta are separated from each other by hundreds of years. Jaimini, the reputed author of the *Pûrva Mimánsa*, is mentioned in the Puránas as the revealer of the Sáma Veda, though we search in vain for any intimation of his name except in what appears to be two interpolated passages in the Grihya-Sutras of the Rig-Veda. Nothing is known of Gautama to whom the Nyáya-Sutras are ascribed. He is said to have been a Kshatriya of the solar race to which king Sudhodana, the father of Buddha, belonged. He is nick-named *Akshapáda*, eye-footed, because he had his eyes always fixed on his feet in abstraction. Kanáda, the word applied to the author of the Vaiseshika, is also a nick-name, meaning " feeder on atoms," in reference to his atomic theory of the Universe. There is nothing known of Patanjali, the supposed author of the Yoga-Sutras. Kapila, the reputed founder of the Sánkhya, is probably a mythical being. Legends represent him to be the son of Brahma, and an incarnation of Vishnu. His name, meaning 'monkey coloured' from Kapi, a monkey, is obviously a nick-name.

Now the question arises—What is the bearing of the Philosophical systems on the deterioration of the Vedic religion, or how did the cultivation of Philosophy contribute to the disintegration of the ancient creed?

The cultivation of Philosophy—when people begin to ask the reason why—marks a stage in the progress of the human mind. For philosophy is an enquiry into the reason of things, into cause and effect, into truth and falsehood; and its fundamental basis is that laid down by the Nyáya, *viz.*, "doubt." When men begin to doubt things which they have been in the habit of blindly believing on authority, and submit everything to the test of reason, the influence of authority must diminish; and in proportion to the correctness of the method pursued in investigation, false notions respecting science and religion must vanish. It often happens, however, that no sooner does the human mind perceive the falsity of its beliefs than it swings to the opposite extreme and denies almost everything! This is precisely what took place in India.

(*a*) The old Vedic-Pantheon is implicitly denied and God is practically ignored! Kapila has no place for Him in his system. Gautama mentions *Isvara*, God, once. Kanáda not at all. Sir Monier Williams says, "Probably the belief of both was that the formation of the world was simply the result of *adrishta*, or unseen force, which is derived from the works, or acts of a previous world, and which becomes in Philosophy a kind of God, if not the only God. Later Náiyaka writers, however, affirm the existence of a supreme Soul, *Paramátman*, distinct from *Jivátman*, or human soul, and this supreme soul is described as eternal, immutable, omniscient, without form, all-pervading, all-powerful, and moreover, as the framer of the Universe."* On this supposition the supreme Soul is not the creator of the world, but at best only a great artificer who may have taken some part in its production from pre-

* Indian Wisdom, p. 85.

existing matter. The *Isvara* of Patanjali, who is described as a *purusha*, or spirit, unaffected by work, is not even the framer of the world, for he adopts the cosmology of Kapila. Jaimini recognizes no authority above that of the Veda. He says 'The Veda is itself authority. Karma, duty, is itself the bestower of reward; and duty consists in the performance of the ritual of the Veda irrespective of any God.' The Vedanta, while affirming the existence of *Isvara*, God, as a practical truth, denies his real existence and resolves all into Brahma. This practical denial of God paved the way for the atheism of Buddha.

(*b*) The Philosophical systems make knowledge the supreme means of liberating the soul from the bondage involved in its union with the body; and thus implicitly deny the authority and utility of the Vedas, though professedly acknowledging both. 'They teach that, though the practice of Vedic ritual may be the means of contributing to final liberation, it cannot effect that end. For it enjoins animal sacrifices and therefore is impure; it is insufficient, since the gods, who attained its highest rewards, perish at the appointed period; and it is excessive, because the happiness of one being is secured at the expense of the good of others.' True knowledge alone gives permanent deliverance and secures an absolute termination to all the ills of human existence.

(*c*) According to the Sánkhya, the soul is devoid of cognition, will, activity, happiness and misery; these belong to the affections of the internal organ, and escape from them is liberation. Now subtract cognition, will, activity, pleasure and pain from the soul, and there is nothing left but a vague entity devoid of all attributes, which is tantamount to nothing. The Nyáya clothes the soul with the attributes denied to it by the Sánkhya, but makes its final liberation, to consist in the loss of the faculties of apprehension, will, and all manifestations of intellectual consciousness.* In what does this differ from practical annihilation? The Vedanta makes the soul identical with Brahma. It has no real existence, but in consequence of the imagination of ignorance, it deludes itself into the belief that it is an entity separate from Brahma, and when this ignorance is removed by studying the Vedánta, it recognizes its identity with Brahma. This prepared the way for the materialism of Buddha.

(*d*) The doctrine of metempsychosis, which appears in some of the Upanishads, is fully developed in all the philosophical systems. Indeed it is the corner-stone of their structure. The commentator on the Sánkhya-Kárika describes souls as animating "animals, deer, birds, reptiles, vegetables and minerals." The Chándogya Upanishad similarly speaks of 'souls entering into wombs as those of a dog, a boar, or a chandála.' The multitude of souls is infinite, and they may inhabit all kinds of forms, from the highest to the lowest. The theory applies even to the gods, for we read, many "thousand Indras have attained not merely heaven, but the sovereignty of heaven; and yet have passed away overcome by time." Activity, whether virtuous or vicious, produces fruits which must be eaten, or effects, the reward of which entails an endless succession of births and deaths, unless the succession be stopped by true

---

* तद्भावश्चाऽपवर्गे तस्य शरीरादेरभावः तदारम्भकधर्माधर्मविरहादिति भावः ॥

Nyàya-Sutra-Vritti, p. 215. Gore's Rational Refutation of the Hindu Philosophical Systems, p. 33.

knowledge; and the object of the systems is to stop the succession by supplying that knowledge.

It is obvious then that the cultivation of Philosophy powerfully contributed to the disintegration of the Vedic religion; for it resulted in the denial of its gods, in making its sacrifices and prayers of none effect, in degrading its priesthood, and in implicitly abrogating caste inasmuch as its plan of salvation by knowledge was open to all. At this stage all that was necessary to the complete overthrow of the ancient faith was to popularise the doctrines of Philosophy, to bring them within the reach of the masses, and to preach them everywhere in the vulgar tongues as the only means of temporal and spiritual happiness. This was done by Sákya-muni, the Buddha.

4.—*The rise of Buddhism.*

Buddhism, emerging naturally from the Philosophical Systems, as they emerged from the Upanishads, gave the death-blow to Vedism and completed the conditions which made the advent of Hinduism possible and necessary.

The founder of Buddhism is so embedded in legends that it is difficult to decide whether he was a real or a mythical person. M. Emile Senart resolves him into a solar myth.* The late Prof. H. H. Wilson doubts that such a person as Buddha ever lived. He points out that there are at least twenty different dates assigned to his birth, varying from 2420 to 453 B.C.† He also dwells on the absurdly extravagant account of his birth given in the *Lalita Vistara.* " After an infinitude of births in various

* Emile Senart—Essai sur la Légend du Buddha.

† Prof. Rhys Davids says that Buddha died within a few years of 412 B.C. Buddhism, p. 213.

characters, during ten million of millions, and one hundred thousand millions of Kalpas,—the shortest of which consists of sixteen millions of years, and the longest of thirty-two millions,—he attained the rank of *Bodhisattva*, that which is inferior only to a Buddha, in the Lushita heaven, where he taught his doctrine to innumerable millions of *Bodhisattvas*, or future Buddhas, and gods and spirits; and was glorified by all the gods and demi-gods of Brahmanical mythology."* In order to rise to the high position of a Buddha one existence more was necessary; he must become incarnate and live on the earth as a man among men. He became incarnate; he was miraculously born from the side of his mother, the beautiful Máyá of the house of Koli, the wife of the King of Kapilavastu. She died seven days after his birth but he was carefully and affectionately brought up by his mother's sister, his father's other wife.

The Royal house of Kapilavastu was an off-shoot of that of Kosala or Oude, and Koli was a similar off-shoot of the Royal house of Varánasi or Benares. These latter principalities were situated in the northern part of Oude, on opposite sides of the river Rohini, a small affluent of the Gogra, about 137 miles to the north of Benares. Prof. H. H. Wilson says that no certain traces of these have been discovered, and that the names of Kapilavastu, Koli, and even the river Rohini, are unknown to modern geography. This was quite true when he wrote, but since then the site of Kapilavastu has been discovered by Dr. Führer in the Nepal Terai about seven miles to the north-west of the Nepal Village of Negliva. In 1898 some of the cremated bones and ashes of Buddha were found in a

---

* Essays on the Religions of the Hindus, Vol. II., p. 345.

Stupa at Piprahwa, a few miles from Kapilavastu. The inscription on a steatite vase among them leaves little doubt that they are the relics of the founder of Buddhism.

Professor H. H. Wilson remarks that the name of Buddha's father, Suddhodana, 'he whose food is pure,' and that of his mother, Máyá, 'illusion,' a name which figures so prominently in the Vedánta Philosophy, suggest fiction rather than fact. He intimates that Kapilavastu, the city of Buddha's birth may be rendered the 'substance of Kapila,' or the Sánkhya Philosophy, on the principles of which Buddha built his system. *

The family name of Buddha was Gautama, the same as that of the founder of the Nyáya Philosophy, and this is the name by which he was known in after life. The titles he assumed, or which were conferred upon him by the pious, are—Buddha, 'the enlightened one'; Siddhártha, 'he by whom the end is accomplished'; Sákya-muni, 'the Sákya sage'; Sákya-sinha, 'the lion of the Sákya tribe'; Sugata, 'the happy one'; Satthá, 'the teacher'; Jina, 'the conqueror'; Bhagaván, 'the blessed one'; Lokanátha, 'the lord of the world'; Sarvajná, 'the omniscient one' and Dharma-rája, 'the king of righteousness.'† Those who adopt the mythical theory of Buddha regard these titles as being very much in the same style as those of the Pilgrim's Progress.

While it cannot be denied that the doctrines of Buddhism might have been developed from the Hindu systems and given to the world under a fictitious name, like that of the Vedánta under the name of Veda-Vyása, there can be no doubt that the mythical theory of Buddha's exist-

* *Ibid*, p. 346.

† Prof. Rhys David's Buddhism, p. 28.

ence is encumbered with more difficulties than that which accepts him as a real historical person. The charm of Buddhism is the *personality* of its founder. It was his *personality* more than his teaching that so amazingly influenced mankind at first, and which continues to influence about five hundred millions of human beings at the present time! His doctrines were more or less scattered in the Philosophical systems; it was the living man that breathed into them the breath of life. It was the benevolence, the love and the self-sacrifice of the *man*, that so profoundly affected his countrymen as to lead them from their own schemes of life into his. The literature of Buddhism has a *person* for its centre; and such monuments as stúpas, topes, dagobas and chaityas have been erected to commemorate the *man* or his relics. A fictitious person, the creation of a dream like Bunyan's Pilgrim, could scarcely have been thus honoured. Besides, it was the *man*, the sympathetic friend, that so endeared himself to mankind that the Bráhmans, in order to counteract his influence and regain their ascendancy, were obliged to bring down the gods from the cold regions of abstraction to the sphere of human affections. Hence the ideas of *incarnation, love* and *faith.* Therefore, making all possible allowance for the accumulation of myths around Buddha, and giving due weight to the later discoveries of the place of his birth and his cremạted remains, we may rest assured that the founder of Buddhism was a *real* and not a fictitious person.

There is not much reliable knowledge about the early life of Gautama. He is represented, on the one hand, as being pensive, retired and averse to the martial adventures of his race; and on the other, as being the chief in all manly sports, distancing all his contemporaries in feats at arms and in mental prowess. He was early married to his cousin, the beautiful Yasodhará, the daughter of the Rájá of Koli. He led a life of pleasure and self-indulgence until the vanity of worldly existence was so impressed upon his mind on four different occasions, by meeting consecutively with a decrepid old man, a sick man, a decaying corpse and a mendicant, that he determined to abandon his royalty and devote himself to the life of an ascetic.

It is scarcely probable, however, that the sight of an old man, or a diseased stranger, or even a dead body, could be sufficient to produce so powerful an effect on one who was not already keenly sensitive to the mysteries of sorrow and death. The fact is that in the midst of luxury and pleasure Gautama felt a craving which nothing could satisfy. Life, therefore, had become insupportable, and he was glad to retire to the forest and live the life of a hermit, which, according to Hindu notions, is free from all perplexities.

In spite of the opposition of his father, he took that step which is called "The great Renunciation." He was about thirty years of age sitting on the river side in one of his pleasure-gardens when the news came that his first and only son, Râhula, was born. He proceeded immediately to the palace determined that this new tie should not prevent his renouncing the world. The auspicious event naturally filled the city of Kapilavastu with joy. As he passed through the streets he was everywhere received with demonstrations of welcome, such as might have shaken a purpose less firm than his; and the congratulations showered upon him as he entered the palace were even more touching. Nevertheless, that night he left his father's house, his young wife, his only child and his wealth, and proceeded to Rájagṛiha, the capital of Mágadha, a great kingdom in the eastern valley of the Ganges. But he had not gone far when Mára, the spirit of evil, appeared in the sky, and urging him to stop, promised to give him in seven days a universal sovereignty over the four continents, if he would give up his enterprise. The tempting offer was scornfully rejected, and the tempter consoled himself with the hope that he might yet overcome him, saying, " Sooner or later some hurtful, or malicious, or angry thought will arise in his mind, in that moment I shall be his master." And from that time 'he followed him like a shadow on the watch for any failing.' Mára is probably only an objective representation of what was then passing through Gautama's mind.

Rájagṛiha was surrounded by hills and forests in the seclusion of which many hermits found it pleasant to reside. There, undisturbed by the outer world, they engaged in meditation and penance for the purpose of solving the great problem of existence, and of obtaining that rest for which their wearied souls longed. Gautama joined them, and, by their assistance, learned all that the Hindu Philosophy had to teach about this world and the next. But he was dissatisfied, his mind was still as restless as the sea. Consequently he retired to the forests of Urúvela, near the present temple of Buddha Gayá, and there for six years, attended by five faithful disciples, devoted himself to the severest penance, abstaining from wholesome food, and subjecting his body to every kind of consecrated torture. The result was a complete prostration of body and mind. He gave up asceticism, took proper food, bathed and walked to Buddha Gayá, and there sat under the famous Bo-tree to complete the work begun and carried on in the midst of so many discouragements. His five disciples forsook him and retired to Benares, for he was now a renegade in their estimation.

When thus alone, disappointed and cast down, his arch enemy, Mára, attacked him again with redoubled fury, calling the elements of nature to his aid, but all his desperate efforts to thwart the emancipation of Sákyamuni were in vain. From early morning until sunset he struggled hard with doubt and despair; but as the day ended doubt and despair vanished, and Gautama became Buddha, the 'enlightened one.' Immediately his face glowed with light and indwelling peace; his eyes beamed with compassion and benevolence; for he had, as he thought, solved the great mystery of suffering; its cause and its cure.

'Buddha had now arrived at those conclusions which from the fundamental doctrines of his system, *viz*:—

(1) There is no God.*

(2) The Vedas are of no authority.

(3) Priests, prayers and sacrifices, are useless.

(4) Caste is a fiction.

(5) There is free salvation to all irrespective of sex, caste, or country.

In this manner he swept away with one stroke the foundations on which the tyranny of the Bráhmans was built, *viz.*, God, the Vedas, Prayers, Sacrifices and Caste.

(6) 'Buddhism has not attempted to solve the problem

* Buddha acknowledged gods as superior sentient beings subject to the law of Karma, but none as objects of worship.

of the origin of things like the Hindu systems of Philosophy. It takes the existence of the natural world and all things therein as an ultimate fact, and holds that every thing is subject to the law of cause and effect. There is no place where this law does not operate. There are celestial worlds where angels dwell, whose existence is more or less material as their previous lives were more or less holy; but the angels die, and the worlds they inhabit pass away. There are hells, where the evil actions of men and of angels produce unhappy beings; but when the active power of the evil which produced them is exhausted, they vanish, for the worlds they inhabit are not eternal.'

(7) We have seen that Kapila, by depriving the soul of cognition, activity and will, reduced it to a virtual nonentity; that the Nyáya by making its beatitude to consist in a state of unconscious sleep like that of a stone degraded it to the level of matter; and that the Vedánta by denying to it any real existence destroyed its individuality. Buddha saw that such a soul was practically useless, and being an atheist, promptly brushed away these cobwebs, and boldly declared that there is no soul.

Man is an assemblage of different properties, or qualities, not one of which corresponds to the idea of soul. There are *material* qualities, *sensations*, abstract *ideas*, *tendencies* of mind, and mental *powers*. But not one of the five aggregates, (*Skandhas*) or any group of them, is permanent. "The first group, *material qualities*," "are like a mass of foam, that gradually forms and then vanishes. The second, the *sensations*, are like a bubble dancing on the face of the water. The third group, the *ideas*, are like the uncertain mirage that appears in the sunshine. The fourth group, the mental and moral *predispositions*, are like a plantain stalk, without firmness or stability. And the last group, the *thoughts*, are like a spectre or magical illusion."*

(8) It is strange that, with the denial of God and the soul, Buddha should have maintained the doctrine of metempsychosis, especially as its truth had never been philosophically demonstrated, but always taken for granted. It is the central doctrine of the Philosophical systems and he could not bring his mind to discard it. In order, however, to bring it into harmony with the denial of God and the soul, it was necessary to modify it. The old doctrine is that the soul, as the result of actions, virtuous or vicious, must pass through various births till the fruit of those actions is exhausted, when it enters into rest. Buddha raised action (Karma) into a kind of objective entity, the procedure of which is inevitable. According to his doctrine of Transmigration, when a man dies the component parts (*Skandhas*) of his material personality dissolve, and a new complex, or being, is formed as the effect of the Karma of the preceding complex, or being. The dissolved component parts of the previous being determine the locality, nature and future of the new being. By this doctrine of Karma, Buddha doubtless intended to maintain the great law of righteous retribution, and to account for the inequalities of the present life. If so, he has utterly failed. For the person who sows and the person who reaps are not identical. The former is the real self and the latter the Karmic self and not the identical ego. Neither good nor evil, therefore, befalls the actor. Hence the chief object

* Prof. Rhys David's Buddhism, p. 93.

of the doctrine is to reduce action to a minimum, and to so exhaust its effects as to leave none to form a new person or Karmic self. The benevolence of the doctrine in this sense is obvious. The pious Buddhist by seeking Nirváṇa is really seeking to avert the calamity of existence from falling on another human being, and thus Buddhism, not only makes annihilation the chief good, but the pursuit of it a pure act of unselfish charity. It is more than probable, however, that the multitudes understood it as eternal repose, or a negative state of consciousness.

These are what we may roughly call the negative conclusions of Buddha, by which he swept away every doctrine of the prevailing creed, except that of Transmigration, which he modified. Had he been a mere destroyer, his influence would not have been greater than that of the *Chárvákas*, an atheistical sect represented by Jáváli in the Rámáyaṇa, whose flippant mocking spirit reminds us of Voltaire. Buddha was a constructor. He claimed to be a prophet, one of a succession, whose object was to lead mankind from sorrow to happiness, from the bonds of sin to final liberation. "Know Vaseṭṭha," he says, in the Tevijja-sutta* "that from time to time a Tathágata is born unto the world, a fully enlightened one, blessed and worthy, abounding in wisdom and goodness, happy, with knowledge of the world, unsurpassed as a guide to every mortal, a teacher of gods and men, a blessed Buddha." "He, by himself, thoroughly understands and sees, as it were face to face, this Universe—the world below with all its spirits, and the world above of Mára and of Brahmá—and all creatures, Sramanas and Bráhmans, gods and men; and he then

* Chap. I. 46.

makes his knowledge known to others. The truth doth he proclaim both in its letter and in its spirit, lovely in its origin, lovely in its progress, lovely in its consummation; the higher life doth he make known in all its purity and in all its perfection."

Buddha's doctrine of suffering, its cause and cure, is similar to that of the Philosophical systems. It is the result of contact between organism and environment—of contact with pleasant and disagreeable objects which leads to desire and aversion, to an eager craving to supply a felt want and a bitter disappointment when the want is not supplied.* The cure consists in walking in the 'Eightfold Path' of a virtuous and thoughtful life.† "Enter on this Path and make an end of sorrow: verily the Path has been preached by me, who have found out how to quench the darts of grief. You yourselves must make the effort, the Buddhas are only preachers: the thoughtful who enter the Path are freed from the bondage of the deceiver Mára."‡

This Path which leads to Nirváṇa, the *summum bonum* of Buddhism, contains:—

| | | | |
|---|---|---|---|
| 1. | Right belief. | 5. | Right life. |
| 2. | Right resolve. | 6. | Right effort. |
| 3. | Right speech. | 7. | Right thinking. |
| 4. | Right act. | 8. | Right meditation.§ |

The meaning of Nirváṇa is going out as of a lamp, extinction, or cessation of existence. Existence *per se* is the greatest evil and cessation from it is the greatest good. When we say cessation from existence, it must be borne in

---

* Dhammacakkappavattana-Sutta, 5, 6.

† *Ibid.*, 8.

‡ Dhammapada, 274—276.

§ Dhammacakkappavattana-Sutta, 4.

mind that it does not mean the cessation of the existence of the soul, for Buddha did not recognize soul. It is, according to Professor Rhys Davids,* 'the extinction of that sinful, grasping condition of mind and heart, which would otherwise, in virtue of the great mystery of *karma*, be the cause of renewed individual existence. When all burning passions and desires are completely subdued, and the mind reposes in a calm peaceful state, feeling nothing, desiring nothing, this is bliss, this is Nirváṇa.' When a man has reached this state he can either live or die as he chooses. Buddha said to Ánanda, "Whosoever has thought out, practised, and ascended to the very heights of the four Paths, to saintship, and so mastered them as to be able to use them as the means of (mortal) advancement, and as a basis for edification—he, should he desire it, would remain in the same birth for a Kalpa, or for that portion of a Kalpa which has yet to run. Now the Tathágata has thought out and thoroughly practised them (in all respects as just now fully described) and might, should he desire it, remain alive for a Kalpa, or for that portion of a Kalpa which has yet to run."†

When the fruit of *karma* is exhausted and the *skandhas*, or aggregates which form the body are dissolved at death, there is nothing to cause the formation of another being, and the Arahat (the holy one) will be no longer alive or existent in any sense whatever, he will have reached Parinibbána, complete extinction. "As a flame, blown by the violence of the wind, goes out and cannot be reckoned as existing, even so a Muni (Saint) delivered from name and form, or body, disappears and cannot be reckoned as existing. For, to him who has disappeared, there is no form

* Buddhism, pp. 111-2.

† Mahá Parinibbána-Sutta, III. 54.

by which they say that he is."* It is evident from these quotations, and many more could be produced, that Nirváṇa is used in two senses—(1) To denote a state of imperturbable repose, unruffled serenity, complete stillness of thought, perfect quietism, which state is attainable in this world. (2) To denote complete extinction of sentient life, the putting out—as the etymology of the word indicates—of the lamp of consciousness, physical and moral annihilation, a state to be attained at death. The first is the flower, the second is the full fruit. Buddha attained the first Nirváṇa under the Bo-tree, and the second when he died.

Gautama, after becoming Buddha, the 'enlightened one', moved by love and pity for humanity, went forth to the deer-park, about three miles north of Benares, "to turn the wheel of the excellent law," which means to preach Dharma, the law which he had formulated, and which he regarded in the same light as Jaimini regarded the Vedas, *viz*., eternal. This Dharma is called Religion, because Hindu thinkers make no distinction between Religion and Philosophy. Strictly speaking, Buddhism is not a Religion but a Philosophy. In the deer-park Buddha met his old disciples who had forsaken him when he abandoned asceticism, and they became his first converts. He preached to all castes without distinction, to the high and the low, to the ignorant and the learned, to men and women, for his law was a law of grace for all. In three months his disciples numbered about sixty, chiefly of the rich youths of Benares; these he sent forth in different directions to preach and great success followed their labours.

* Sutta—Nipáta, Páráyanavagga, 7. 6.

Buddha spent the greater part of every year in travelling from place to place, preaching constantly and adding to the number of his disciples. During the four rainy months only he remained in one place, instructing his followers, and framing rules for the guidance of his Saṅgha, or monastic order.

This order was one of the chief factors which contributed to the rapid progress of Buddhism, for all castes of both sexes were admitted into it, and all who entered it were allowed to beg their food and live on charity. The spirit of benevolence had been so abundantly infused into all Buddhists that the rich gave freely towards the support of the poor in general, and the monks and nuns in particular. Any system that would promise salvation to the rich for supplying the necessities of the poor, the idle and the priests, would soon conquer India to-day!

The monks and nuns had to take the vow of poverty and chastity, and of obedience to the commandments not to kill, not to steal, not to lie, not to taste intoxicating drinks, not to eat at forbidden times, not to attend theatrical amusements, not to use garlands and perfumes in dressing, not to sleep on any soft material. The first five are binding on all who profess Buddhism, and the whole ten on those who have entered the order and are walking in the 'Eightfold Path.'

The contact of the Aryans with the aboriginal inhabitants, the action and reaction of the religion of the one on the religion of the other, and the cultivation of philosophy, had prepared the masses for the acceptance of Buddhism. The political condition of India, at the time, was also favourable to the success of that system. The old Kshatriya clans, who were under Bráhmanical influence were breaking up, and great kingdoms were founded by mighty conquerors, many of whom belonged to the lower classes. When Buddhism, therefore, abolished the distinction of caste, denounced the tyranny of the priests, pronounced the constant call for bloody sacrifices a crime, and proclaimed good-will and benevolence to all classes in the vulgar tongues, it spread like wild fire all over India. In the life-time of Buddha, Bindusára, the most powerful Rájá in the Ganges valley, became a Buddhist, and probably his example was followed by his subjects. His wife, Kshemá, entered the order of nuns. Buddhism was publicly proclaimed by the Emperor Asoka as the national religion of India about the end of the third century B. C. "In less than two years," says he, "the gods who were worshipped in Jambudvípa (India) have been rendered false; and this result is not the effect of my greatness but of my zeal." Kanishka, who flourished about the beginning of the Christian era, and whose dominions extended nearly all over India, was a zealous Buddhist. *But Nemesis was at hand.*

---

## CHAPTER II.

### The Reaction of the Bráhmans.

1.—*The Bráhmanical lever.*

The Bráhmans did not look on calmly when their system was overturned and their power destroyed. They set themselves resolutely to stem the torrent and ultimately prevailed. They held a mighty power in their hands which all the enthusiasm for humanity manifested by Buddha could not withstand in the long run. They supplied the people with objects of worship which the cold atheism of

Buddha had taken away. Well did they characterise Buddhism as *Súnyaváda*, the 'system of the void.' Man cannot live on such a system, for the negation of God does violence to the most sacred instincts of his nature. Atheism was the destruction of Buddhism, and Deism or Polytheism was the conquest of the Bráhmans. Indeed in countries where Buddhism is professed, the people try to satisfy the cravings of their nature for God by worshipping images and supposed relics of the founder. Buddha's ashes had scarcely become cold when he was elevated into a god and adored as an incarnation. The Buddhists of Ceylon believe in devil worship and in the power of the stars; the Buddhists of China worship heaven as the Supreme, and the spirits of ancestors as inferior deities. In the time of Fa-Hian, the Buddhists of North India worshipped, along with the image of Buddha, two *Bodhisatwas*, or future Buddhas, called *Manjusri* and *Avalokitesvara;* and the Nepalese in the tenth century A. D., invented a deity which they named Ádi-Buddha, or primordial Buddha, the self-existent one.

The Jains of the Dekhan, who are probably an off-shoot from Buddhism, have invented *Jinapati*, or supreme Jina, whom they worship; Jina, conqueror, being one of the names of Buddha.

2.—*The Bráhmanical tactics.*

The Bráhmans were unable to restore the ancient creed in its entirety. They saw that the old gods were too impersonal and distant to attract the multitude who felt the glow of Buddha's personality, sympathy and love. They saw that the old difference between the Aryans and the aborigines had to a great extent been banished, for many Bráhmans belonged to Buddha's Saṅgha, and some of the most powerful kings were low caste. What was to be done? They adopted the policy of 'give and take.' They effected a compromise between the aboriginal cults and the Aryan beliefs; emphasizing the *human* side; hence the doctrines of Incarnation and Emanation. They gave prominence to two gods, Vishṇu and Siva, the chief characteristic of the former being incarnations, and of the latter the worship of sex. They clothed these with the attributes of the Vedic and aboriginal gods recognised by both parties. They clustered around them, in the Epics and Puráṇas, all the stories of gods, demons and heroes, which were likely to touch the heart or inflame the passions. And thus they gradually built up what is now known as Hinduism, a stupendous system which banished Buddhism from India, and re-established the dominion of the Bráhmans and the tyranny of caste. The Bráhmans, however, gave up bloody sacrifices and adopted Buddha's doctrine of *Ahiṁsá*, not killing; consequently the royal sacrifices of Rájasúyá and Asvamedha were not restored. But those who desired to offer bloody sacrifices were at liberty to do so.

3.—*The Bráhmanical triumph.*

In the time of Fa-Hian, the Chinese pilgrim, 339—414 A.D.,* the tide against the Buddhists was rising, for he says that they were well-nigh driven from Kanouj and Kosala. In the city of Kanouj there were only two Saṅghárámas, monasteries; and in Kosala the Bráhmans persecuted the Buddhists, destroyed their buildings, and built a temple to the gods close to a Buddhist chapel. A little more than two hundred years later, 629—645 A. D.,† Hiouen-Thsang.

* Talboys Wheeler's History of India, Vol. III., Chap. V., pp. 243—259.
† *Ibid.*, pp. 259—281. Prof. Rhys David's Buddhism, pp. 243—247.

another Chinese pilgrim, visited India. He testified that almost everywhere Buddhism was on the wane and Hinduism on the increase. He came to Peshwar when it was ruled by Kapisa and saw many Buddhist monasteries and stúpas, including many a monument built by Asoka and Kanishka, in ruins. The multitude of temples showed the prevalence of Hinduism in association with the worship of Ísvara or Siva. Hiouen-Thsang proceeded northwards to Udyána where most of the Buddhist monasteries were in ruins. He entered Kashmere which was ruled by a king who favoured Hinduism. Proceeding southward to Mathurá and Tamsar, he found that Hinduism was at least as prevalent as Buddhism. The pilgrim next went to Ayodhyá where Buddhism was struggling for life, and thence to Prayága where Hinduism was flourishing. Kapilavastu, the birth-place of Gautama, was in ruins; and Hinduism was in the ascendànt at Kausambi, Srávasti and Benares. Going to Mágadha, he found 50 Buddhist monasteries with ten thousand monks; but Hindu temples were also numerous and well attended. Páṭaliputra had fallen into ruins since the visit of Fa-Hian, and Hiouen-Thsang counted hundreds of broken down monasteries, stúpas and pagodas. Gayá was a well defended city, thickly populated, but among its population there were a thousand Bráhman families. Ancient Rájagriha was in ruins, but there was a new city occupied by many Bráhmans.

In his travels through eastern Hindustan, Hiouen-Thsang came to Champá, the modern Bhagulpore, where Buddhism was declining and Hinduism flourishing. At Pundia-Kardhana, probably Burdwan, there were twenty Buddhist monasteries and a hundred Hindu temples. In

Assam he found hundreds of temples attended by thousands of worshippers. From Assam he proceeded apparently to the Sunderbands and thence to Tamraliptra, or Tamluk, where he saw ten monasteries and fifty temples. On his way to the south, he found that Orissa contained a hundred monasteries and five temples, and Kaliṅga on the coast, ten monasteries and two hundred temples. Buddhism, however, prevailed at Káñchípuram, the modern Conjeeveram, for there were a hundred monasteries with ten thousand monks, and only eighty temples. From Conjeeveram he crossed to the western coast known as Malabar, and then returned towards the north through Travancore. There the monasteries were in ruins and hundreds of temples flourishing. In the Konkan there were about as many temples as monasteries. In Mahárásh̤tra Hinduism predominated; and in Malwa Buddhism and Hinduism were both equally prosperous. The king of Vallabhí was a zealous Buddhist; but in both Ujjain and Chittore Buddhism was being superseded by Hinduism. Turning away westward the pilgrim passed through the gloomy desert of Marwar towards Scinde where he found the king a Súdra, and Buddhism in the ascendant. In Multan Buddhism had been superseded by the worship of the sun. Besides, he passed through many unknown kingdoms where Buddhism and Bráhmanism seemed to have been nearly balanced, and at last he made his way over the Hindu-kush into his own country.

It is now obvious that in the time of Hiouen-Thsang Buddhism was not the powerful religion it had been in the days of Fa-Hian, and even then it had passed its zenith. It was equal to Hinduism only where it was supported by the secular arm. It was recognised as the national religion only in Kashmere and the Upper Punjab, in Mágadha and Guzerat. In the eighth and ninth centuries of our era it had become very corrupt; and active opposition to it was stimulated by the learned Bráhmans Kumárila Bhaṭṭa and Saṅkarácharya. In the eleventh century A.D., Harshadeva, king of Kashmir, supported Buddhism; but in the twelfth century, when the Muhammadans conquered Kashmir, there were no Buddhists left in India excepting a few who preserved an ignoble existence by joining the Jains, and conforming outwardly to Hindu customs and ceremonial observances. Thus the Bráhmans by means of Hinduism conquered India and the Buddhists became extinct!

Perhaps some may think that as a factor in the disintegration of Vedism Jainism should be mentioned. Jainism, however, is probably an off-shoot of Buddhism,* and so very much like the latest phase of it that, for the purpose of this Dissertation, it is not necessary to consider it.

---

* Should Jacobi's opinion to the contrary be true, it is immaterial in this case.

# PART II.

## The Edifice.

"All history is the search after God."—*Lyman Abbott.*

"Don't imagine that you understand a people if you have not pushed your enquiry to their gods."—*Quinet.*

"The further one advances into the labyrinth of Hindu religion, the more superstition, the more devils, demons, magic, witchcraft and uncanny things generally, does he find."—*Hopkins.*

It was stated in the previous Part that Hinduism is the fusion of corrupt Vedic doctrines with non-Aryan aboriginal cults; and that it contains all the religious beliefs and practices of modern India. The factors which made that fusion possible and necessary were also pointed out. We now proceed to consider the component parts of Hinduism, and show how they were evolved from disintegrated fragments of Vedism and non-Aryan cults. The component parts of Hinduism are,—(i) Gods, (ii) Goddesses, (iii) Worship, and (iv) Philosophy. Our task, therefore, in this Part is to enquire what elements—Aryan and non-Aryan—entered into the constitution of each of these, and so to bring within view the manner in which Hinduism was built up.

---

### CHAPTER I.

### I. THE GODS.

1.—*The Trimúrti.*

The tendency to associate the gods in groups of three is visible in the Hymns of the Vedas. The idea is often expressed in the Bráhmaṇas that there are three gods, Agni,

Váyu, and Súrya, *i.e.*, a god for the earth, fire; another for the atmosphere, wind; and a third for the heaven, sun. Yáska, an old etymologist, reproduces this division and resolves all the gods into one or other of the three.*

The Hindu triad is composed of Brahmá, Vishṇu and Siva, denoting the functions of creation, preservation and destruction. The Sectaries resolve all the three into their chief preferential god. Thus the Vaishṇavas declare that Vishṇu is both Brahmá and Siva; and the Saivas similarly maintain that Siva is both Brahmá and Vishṇu. Hence the votaries of either sect, when addressing their principal god, begin by uttering the sacred syllable OM, which is a combination of the letters A U M representing Vishṇu, Siva and Brahmá, as the three in one.

2.—*Brahma.*

Bráhman in the neuter gender signifies prayer in the oldest portions of the Vedas; and in the masculine, "he of prayer," the priest or the Bráhman, 'the utterer of prayer *par excellence.* Prayer was supposed to be sufficiently powerful to constrain the most intractable god to grant whatever boon the suppliant desired; and hence it naturally developed into the Supreme Being. In the latter portions of the Vedas, it grew into the absolute, the abstract of all existences, the *Satya*, the only true reality.† Brahma in this capacity is *nirguṇa*, without attributes or any such characteristics as constitute a conscious personal being; and in this sense it has continued to be the

* The same classification is found among the two leading nations of antiquity, the Chaldeans and the Egyptians. The Chaldean triad was formed of Anu, Bel and Ea, representing the heaven, the lower world and the water; the Egyptian of Tum, Ra and Kheper, or of Osiris, Isis and Horus.

† Phillip's Teaching of the Vedas, pp. 77—80.

expression of the highest generalization of Philosophy.* On the popular side, it developed into the concrete male god, Brahmá, *saguṇa*, with attributes. In the Rámáyaṇa and Mahábhárata, which in their present form were composed for the promotion of Hinduism, Brahmá occupies the throne of the Universe, and is addressed as the "grand sire," the "guardian," and the "refuge of gods and men." But even in the Epics his glory is perceptibly on the wane before the rising splendour of Vishṇu and Siva. In the Puráṇas he is altogether superseded by these deities, or merged into the one or the other; his name being retained in the Trimúrti as a relic of his former greatness.

When Brahmá was supreme among the gods, he was identified with Prajápati of the Vedas, and the legends current about that god were transferred to him. As Prajápati was born from an egg in the primeval waters in order to turn chaos into kosmos, so Brahmá was born in the same way for the same purpose. As Prajápati assumed the form of a tortoise in order to create progeny and blessed the boar that raised the earth, so Brahmá, at the time of the deluge, assumed the form of a fish and as a boar raised up the earth from the great waters. Hence he was called Náráyaṇa, 'he who moves on the waters,' a name which afterwards became the distinguishing title of Vishṇu. As Prajápati conceived an unholy desire for his

* मन्मते ब्रह्मणो द्रव्यत्वासिद्धेः । गुणाश्रयत्वं समवायिकारणत्वं वा द्रव्यत्वमिति तेऽभिमतं नहि निर्गुणस्य ब्रह्मणो गुणाश्रयता नाऽपि समवायिकारणता समवायासिद्धेः ॥

Vedánta Paribhásha, p. 18. Gore's Rational Refutation of the Hindu Philosophical System, p. 176.

daughter, the sky, so Brahmá sought incestuous intercourse with his daughter, Vác; for which Siva cursed him; in consequence he lost one of his five heads, and was ever after known as *Caturmukha,* the four-faced one.*

An attempt was made by the more conservative Bráhmans of the "Reaction" to revive the worship of Brahmá and to restore the ancient creed as it was before the schism of Buddha. When Buddhism was defeated,—though not destroyed—the followers of Vishṇu and Siva, who had fought unitedly against the common foe, began to fight with each other for supremacy. The Puráṇas give expression to that rivalry. This afforded an opportunity to the votaries of Brahmá to assert his claims. For this purpose they compiled the Code of Manu which synchronizes with the rise of Hinduism. Manu is a mythical person, like Vyása, to whom all floating precepts, the authors of which were unknown, are ascribed. The compilers of the Code were Bráhmans of the most orthodox school. Hence they tried to restore the hard and fast line of caste in all its ramifications, and the supremacy and tyranny of the Bráhmans in all their fulness. The religion of the Code is Bráhmanism pure and simple as it existed in pre-Buddhistic days. The old gods of the Vedas are acknowledged, but Brahmá is the supreme Being.† Public sacrifices are mentioned, but the chief rites of religion are of a domestic character resembling those of Vedic times. Vishṇu and Siva and their wives, Lakshmí and Bhadrakálí, are known, but

---

* The germs of this legend are found in Rig Veda, X. 61, 5-9, but are too indecent for translation.

† Manu, IX. 303.

only once mentioned.* Temples, idols, and Bráhmans in charge are spoken of; but only for the purpose of denunciation. Nevertheless, the temples and idols of Vishṇu and Siva had laid such a hold on the masses that the compilers of the Code felt bound to enact laws for their protection.† But the promulgation of the Code and all the efforts put forth to popularize Brahmá failed; because, (1) he was too abstract and distant to attract the multitudes who had fallen under the spell of Buddha's personality; (2) he was too well-known as the chief god of Bráhmanism to be brought down and fused with the animal gods of the aborigines and the hero gods of the Aryans. He has therefore almost ceased to be an object of worship in India. Pushkara in Ajmere is the only place where he is addressed by his thousand names and adored by means of a ritual similar to that which obtains in the temples of Vishṇu and Siva.

The real reason of the eclipse of Brahmá by Vishṇu and Siva being unknown, a legend was devised to account for it; and, at the same time, to show the superiority of these gods over the great God of Bráhmanism.

There was a dispute, we are told, between Brahmá and Vishṇu as to which was the greatest; He as the creator or Vishṇu as the preserver. Both appealed to Siva. Siva decided that the one should ascend and ascertain the height of the linga and the other descend and ascertain its depth; the first to return after accomplishing his task to be considered the greatest. Thereupon Brahmá ascended and Vishṇu descended, but the one could neither ascertain its height nor the other its depth. Brahmá, however, declared, on his return, that he had

* *Ibid.*, XII. 121; III. 80. † *Ibid.*, III. 152, 180; IV. 39, 130; VII. 67.

ascertained its height and called the sacred flower Kétakí to support his statement. Siva, knowing that he was guilty of falsehood, cursed him, the effect of which was to deprive him of worship. Against this he remonstrated, and Siva allowed his worship on auspicious occasions, such as Soma sacrifices and initiatory ceremonies.

The four-faced Brahmá is represented in pictures and sculptures with a crown on each of his heads. From his four heads the four Vedas are said to have proceeded. On his forehead he wears a painted mark of three horizontal lines with a round dot about the size of a shilling in the centre; his hair locks are decorated with strings of pearls; and in his four hands he holds respectively the Vedas, a sacrificial ladle, a rosary and an earthen water-pot. His colour is tawny. He sits on a lotus, and rides on a swan.

The Devil-worshippers of south India, who have partly absorbed him into their cult, represent him as a demon in human form with matted hair, riding furiously, sword in hand, on a swift horse to drive away evil spirits. The people of the western coast, especially the Tulus, worship him as a devil and thus invoke him,—"We have been remiss in thy worship, spare us; remove graciously from us all evil, give us health for our body; increase our wealth in the house and in the field." And the Bráhman priest after performing the usual ceremonies says:—"I reverence the sunlike, three-eyed Náráyaṇa, who is shining with the ornament of the serpent prince, who is honored by the skull held in his hand, who is armed with a chisel and a white lotus, who has anklets with golden bells and who is now facing me, the lord of the bhútas (devils), who removes fear, has four faces and is called Brahmá."

There is a popular legend that one of the four heads of

Brahmá which Siva cut off became united with a *nágadeva*, serpent god.

*Vidhi*, destiny, is a universal doctrine in India. Brahmá is believed to write on the forehead of every individual all that will befall him in this life and in that to come. This *Vidhi* accounts for all actions, whether good or evil, and hence the actors are irresponsible!

Brahmá, with the exception of the effort made to identify him with the devils and the serpent gods of the aborigines, has remained an Aryan deity. But his evolution as such has been in the wrong direction, downwards and not upwards. First, he was an abstraction of the power behind prayer which responds to the suppliant's cry; then he developed into the concrete male Brahmá, the creator of all things, whom Vishṇu and Siva adored; later he became the equal of Vishṇu and Siva in the Trimúrti; afterwards he degenerated into an incestuous liar with whom the most voluptuous Rájá could scarcely compete, and became a devil; and lastly he coalesced with an animal, a *nága*, and blossomed into a serpent god!

3.—*Vishṇu.*

Vishṇu, from root *vish* to work, to shine, to pervade, is the second person in the Hindu triad; but the religion of Vishṇu is probably of later date than that of Siva, the third person.

In the Vedas Vishṇu is a sun-god representing that luminary in its rising, culmination and setting; and hence one of his many names is *Trivikrama*, 'one who strides the three steps.' He is said to have established the heaven and the earth; to contain all worlds in his strides; to have made, in conjunction with Indra, the atmosphere wide, stretched out the earth, produced the sun, the dawn and the fire; to have received the homage of Varuṇa; and in Rig-veda VII. 99, 2, his greatness is said to have no limits within the present or the future. 'He is a personification of the sacrifice, and in this respect the hymns speak of his violent death, a feature which agrees well with a solar-deity, and which occurs again in the final catastrophe that befell Krishṇa, his ninth incarnation.'*

The high attributes ascribed to Vishṇu in many prayers, if they stood alone, are such as to lead to the conclusion that he was considered one of the chief gods by the old Bards. But the small number of hymns in which he is exclusively, or pre-eminently magnified, compared with those in which the great gods, Indra, Agni and Varuṇa, are celebrated, show that he occupied but an inferior place in the cultus. Besides, in the texts where he is most highly magnified, he is associated with Indra, and is said to have made his three strides by the power of that deity. He is always the faithful friend and companion of Indra both in his wars with the demons of darkness and drought, and in his excessive drinking of the intoxicating Soma juice.

The root conception of Vishṇu is that of a benevolent god, ever ready to descend into the earth and assume different natures and forms in order to succour the oppressed and to restore ṛighteousness and peace among men. It is true that in his incarnations, especially in that of Krishṇa, this conception is obscured, but this is just what might have been expected under the operation of the law of deterioration dominant in Hindu religious thought.

The Vishṇu cult originated *after* the rise of Buddhism with the object of counteracting that system. It

---

* Barth's Religions of India, p. 166.

began obscurely and proceeded slowly, gathering momentum as it moved along. But we have no means of ascertaining when it commenced to assume importance and to command the attention and adherence of the masses. The fact that in the Code of Manu Vishṇu is only once mentioned is no proof that he was not a dramatic god at the time of its promulgation; for the compilers, whose object was to re-establish the cult of Brahmá, would naturally give no prominence to a rival, whether Vishṇu or Siva. It is generally understood that Krishṇa is the Hercules mentioned by Megasthenes, the Greek envoy at the Court of Páṭaliputra, as being worshipped by the inhabitants of the Ganges valley at the beginning of the third century before Christ. That might be true without the implication that he was *then* fused with Vishṇu and regarded as an incarnation of that deity; for there is a strong probability that he was a hero worshipped as a *kula-deva*, ethnic god, by some Aryan tribes before he was merged in the Vishṇu cult.

The question then arises—How did Vishṇu who occupies but an inferior place in the Vedas become supreme,—a position which he has maintained for ages among about one-half of the inhabitants of India? There is but one answer—*By means of the doctrine of incarnations, or descents.*

There are vague adumbrations of this doctrine in the Vedas. The gods often merge into one another. Agni is Indra, Indra is Súrya, and these again are all the gods. Varuṇa is personified as a great king; Indra is called a bull, and Rudra a wild boar. Vishṇu is a manifestation of the three stations of the sun in the sky. Prajápati assumed the form of a tortoise; Brahmá became a fish and a boar and was, besides, in the *abstract* identified with all things. There is but a short step from this to the doctrine that the deity, in the *concrete*, enters an animal or a man, and becomes incarnate therein.

The doctrine of metempsychosis, which is older than Buddha, is also suggestive of the doctrine of incarnations. There is every probability that metempsychosis was derived from the aboriginal inhabitants. For, as Professor Macdonell says, "The Rig Veda contains no traces of it beyond a couple of passages in the last book which speak of the soul of a dead man as going to the waters or plants. It is scarcely credible that such a doctrine could have originated in the stray fancies of one or two poets. It seems more probable that the Aryan settlers received the first impulse in this direction from the aboriginal inhabitants of India. As is well-known, there is among half savage tribes a widespread belief that the soul after death passes into the trunk of trees and the bodies of animals. Thus the Santhals of India are said, even at the present day, to hold that the souls of the good enter into fruit-bearing trees. But among such races the notion of transmigration does not go beyond a belief in the continuance of human existence in animals and trees."* Whether the last sentence is true or not, it is certain from the Upanishads and post-vedic literature that the Aryan invaders believed metempsychosis to include moral retribution, and that the result was the *ascent* of the virtuous soul into union with the Supreme Soul. Now, if the souls of men, which, philosophically are emanations from the deity, descended into the bodies of animals, or ascended into union with the Supreme Soul, it is evident that a little expansion of

* Sanskrit Literature, pp. 387-8.

the doctrine would inevitably bring down the Supreme Soul into animals and human beings. And this is precisely what seems to have taken place among the aborigines before the advent of the Aryans. For there is no reason to suppose that they did not believe *then* what they believe *now*, *viz.*, that a superhuman power, demon, or spirit, dwells in each of the animals they worship, and in curious stones and remarkable trees which command their homage.

Again, the doctrine of incarnations was prevalent among the Akkadians, with whom the Turanian aborigines of India are supposed to have affinity. The Akkadian Eakin (*Ea*, the fish) is the god of the deep, and is identical with the Chaldean Oanes mentioned by Berossos. The fish-god Oanes conceals under his fishy form a human body with a human head and feet, and speaks with a human voice. He has assumed from time to time many forms or incarnations which are called *Annedotoi*. Eakin is the creator of the Akkadians who call themselves the "black people," a designation which the aborigines of south India also apply to themselves in the Tamil and Telugu languages. His weapon was the disc which is also that of Vishṇu. If the conjecture be true that the aborigines of India belong to the same race as the Akkadians it follows that the root idea of the incarnations of Vishṇu was derived from them.* Further, if we could be sure that the incarnations ascribed to Buddha were *prior* to those ascribed to Vishṇu, it would be an additional proof of the Gouda-Dravidian source of the doctrine. For Buddha owed his success chiefly to the antagonism between the ruling Aryans and the depressed aborigines, whose cause he championed, and with whom he fraternized. But unfor-

* Bháratavarsha, pp. 327-8.

tunately the date of the Buddhist Scriptures is at present too uncertain to warrant the inference that the incarnations ascribed to Buddha were prior to those ascribed to Vishṇu. However, the balance of probability seems to be on the side of the supposition that the doctrine of incarnations was derived from the non-Aryan aborigines of India.

The adoption of this doctrine by the Bráhmans and the dexterous use they made of it are quite consistent with their invariable sagacity. Buddhism, which appealed to the masses, had broken their power and destroyed their gods. They felt it necessary in self-defence to take advantage of the godward tendency of the human mind to furnish the people with more popular deities than those of the ancient creed. And this they accomplished in the case of Vishṇuism, by amalgamating the Vedic Vishṇu with the chief animals and fetishes worshipped by the aborigines, and the chief heroes revered by the Aryans; and in the case of Sivaism by identifying the Vedic Rudra with the demons, liṅga-fetish and some animals worshipped by the aborigines.

The key to this theory is the absorption of Buddha into the Vishṇu cult by making the arch-heretic an incarnation of Vishṇu.* Buddha, notwithstanding his denial of God, was adored as a god by multitudes who were naturally hostile to the new religion of Vishṇu. It was necessary therefore by conciliation to bring them over to the new faith. This was done by the bold declaration that Buddha was an incarnation of Vishṇu. In like manner it was affirmed that the animal gods of the aborigines and the

* मत्स्यः कूर्मो वराहश्च नारसिंहश्च वामनः ।
रामो रामश्च रामश्च कृष्णो बुद्धो जनार्दनः ॥

heroes, or demi-gods of the Aryans, were incarnations of him.

Vishṇu became incarnate successively in the fish, the tortoise, the boar and the lion; and in the heroes Vámana, Parasuráma, Ráma, Krishṇa and Buddha. The myths by which these incarnations are represented, while possessing a substratum of historical truth, are chiefly Bráhmanical embellishments for the purpose of connecting Vishṇu with the popular animal and hero worship.

The first three incarnations seem to be based on some traditions of a universal deluge. For in the fish, Vishṇu became incarnate in order to save Manu, the Indian Noah, from the deluge; in the tortoise to recover certain valuable articles lost by the deluge; and in the boar to deliver the world from the power of the demon, Hiraṇyáksha, who had seized the earth and hurled it into the lowest depth of the sea; or according to another legend, to recover the lost Vedas from the great waters. Vishṇu became incarnate in the lion to destroy the demon, Hiraṇyakasipu, who having usurped the dominion of the three worlds, appropriated the sacrifices made to the gods, and threatened to destroy his pious son, Prahláda, for praising Vishṇu.

The four animals in which Vishṇu became incarnate are gods of the aborigines. The fish-god, half man and half fish, has received the homage and adoration of other nations besides the Hindus. The tortoise and the boar are still worshipped in India. The former by the Garus, a people dwelling between Assam and Bengal; and the latter by a very degraded tribe inhabiting a district south-east of Ajmere. The lion has well nigh become extinct in India, but he figures largely in Hindu literature and sculpture, and must have been a very popular god at one time.

In the Vámana, or dwarf, incarnation, Vishṇu was born as the son of the sage Kâsyapa, the younger brother of Indra, and his wife Aditi. He assumed the form of a Bráhman dwarf for the purpose of destroying the demon, Bali, who resembles Kaṁsa in the Krishṇa legend. Appearing before the demon as a diminutive man he asked, as a boon, for as much land as he could step in three paces. Bali, thinking the request exceedingly modest, readily granted it. But to his horror the dwarf immediately expanded himself into such enormous dimensions as to stride over heaven and earth in two steps, leaving Pátála (lower regions) only in the possession of the demon! In the Parasuráma incarnation Vishṇu was born as the son of Jamadagni, a descendant of the great sage Bhṛigu, for the purpose of punishing the Kshatriyas who had cruelly oppressed the Bráhmans. Vishṇu became Ráma to slay Rávaṇa the monster King of Ceylon; and Krishṇa to overthrow the wicked tyrant Kaṁsa. He was born as Buddha to delude the Daityas, demons or masses, to expose themselves to certain destruction by neglecting the worship of the gods. In the last incarnation, that of the Kalki or the horse, Vishṇu will be born in the family of Vishṇu-yazas, an ancient Bráhman, to destroy wickedness and re-establish righteousness in the earth. This conception originated naturally in the hopelessness of sin-suffering humanity to save itself without the intervention of the deity. The form, a Bráhman riding on a white horse, is also natural to the Hindu mind; for a Bráhman is the highest Hindu type of a man, and the horse was an animal highly prized in ancient times; the horse-sacrifice being considered the most efficacious.*

* Phillip's Teaching of the Vedas, pp. 196—8.

The dwarf incarnation probably represents the contests between the Aryans and the aborigines when the former were imposing their religion upon the latter. In Parasuráma we see the Bráhmans crushing the rising power of the Kshatriyas and establishing their own supremacy. Ráma, the son of Dasaratha, represents the extension of Aryan power and civilization from north to south India. Krishṇa shows the high state of development attained in the sphere of politics while religion at the same time degenerated into the lowest depth of infamy. The popular reaction against Bráhmanical tyranny is manifest in Buddha. Some legends substitute Balaráma, the brother of Krishṇa, for Buddha; and some give the number of incarnations as twenty-four and even greater.*

Vishṇuism owes more to Krishṇa than to all the other incarnations. He was the chief factor in its formation and has continued to be its chief support in every age. Parasuráma, being a Bráhman and the champion of his caste against the Kshatriyas, could scarcely by fusion with Vishṇu be made an acceptable god to the ruling and middle classes. The hero of the Rámáyaṇa, though a Kshatriya, was too high-minded, chivalrous and moral, to make Vishṇuism palatable to a sensual people. He was the best type of the husband and the householder, but was too cold and distant to inspire warm devotion and impassioned love. Krishṇa, on the other hand, possessed all the qualifications necessary to command the homage and inflame the love of a people steeped in carnality. He was intensely human, the friend of all, sharing in the games and pleasures of the peasants in the fields as well as in the weightier matters of kings and warriors in the senate and the camp.

---

* Bháratavarsha, p. 310.

Krishṇa* was the son of Vasudeva and Devakí, descendants of Yadu. Devakí was the cousin of Kaṁsa, the king of Mathurá. Kaṁsa, while driving the bride and bridegroom home after the nuptial ceremony, heard a voice from heaven, saying:—"O Kaṁsa, the eighth son of Devakí will be thy destroyer." Thereupon, he, in great wrath, seized Devakí by her hair, drew his sword, and would have killed her on the spot, had not Vasudeva assured him that no son of his should ever hurt him. Fearing, however, that the prophecy would be fulfilled, he imprisoned Vasudeva and Devakí in the palace, and killed their first six children! The seventh, Balaráma, was abstracted from his mother's womb, transferred to that of Rohiṇí, the second wife of Vasudeva, and thus was saved. The eighth was Krishṇa, the "black one." His name seems to indicate that he belonged to the aboriginal inhabitants, or at any rate that he was not a pure Aryan. The Bráhman editors of the Mahábhárata saw this difficulty and endeavoured to meet it by affirming that he was formed from a "black hair" of Vishṇu as Balaráma had been from a "white one."

Krishṇa was born on a rainy night, when the low pleasing sounds of a tropical down-pour lulled the guards of the palace to sleep. Vasudeva placed the child in a basket and carried it over the river Jumna to conceal it from Kaṁsa. The river was swollen, but at the touch of Krishṇa's foot, it became shallow. As the rain fell in torrents, *Seshanága,* the many-headed serpent, followed Vasudeva and canopied the father and the child with his stupendous hood. On the other side of the Jumna,

* Cf. Windisch, Ueber das Drama Mṛcchakatika und die Krichna legende, pp. 445—466.

Vasudeva found the waggon and team of the herdsman, Nanda, whose wife, Yasodá, had just been delivered of a daughter. He took the infant in exchange for Krishṇa and secretly conveyed her to Devakí. The child cried and the guards were roused. The news of the birth was carried to Kaṁsa who rushed furiously to the house of Vasudeva to kill the babe; it however ascended calmly to heaven, saying, "A son is born who will destroy the house of Kaṁsa!" Therefore Kaṁsa, Herod-like, ordered all infants to be slain throughout the land in the hope of compassing the death of Krishṇa. Meanwhile, Nanda took his wife and the child to his home at Gokula, where Krishṇa amused himself with all sorts of childish frolics. One day he upset the waggon in which his foster father and mother dwelt and broke the pots and pans. He often went to the cowpens and teased the calves by pulling their tails. As he grew, the spirit of mischief grew within him. He upset his mother's butter-churn and stole the butter from the milk-maids. Once when the milk-maids were bathing in the Jumna he took away their clothes, and climbing up a tree made each damsel come out of the water and receive her garments from his hands! In consequence of his naughtiness his foster mother fastened a rope round his waist, and tied him to a wooden mortar used for pounding rice, and angrily said, "Now, you naughty boy, get away from there if you can." She had no sooner departed to her work than he pulled the mortar to the space between two large trees in front of the house, and being wedged between them, he continued to pull till they fell with a crash which frightened all the villagers! Regarding this as a bad omen the villagers left Gokula and went with their cattle to Vrindávana.

There Krishṇa roamed in the woods with the Gopís, (cowherdesses) who devoted themselves body and soul to him. Decking his locks with peacock's feathers he sported and danced with them, played the flute day and night for their amusement, and became such a favourite with them that they considered every moment in his company worth myriads of years!

The inhabitants of Vrindávana were worshippers of Indra until Krishṇa persuaded them to present their offerings to the mountain Govardhana which supplied grass to their cattle. Indra was greatly offended at the loss of his offerings and in revenge attempted to destroy the people by a deluge. Krishṇa frustrated his efforts by holding up the mountain on his finger, like an umbrella, to shelter them.

When still a boy, Krishṇa killed the child-destroyer *Pútaná* and the great serpent-fiend *Káliya*. After growing up he killed many demons and conquered many enemies in war. At the invitation of Kaṁsa, who had planned his destruction, he came on a visit to Mathurâ, and on entering the city killed the washerman of the king and arrayed himself in the stolen garments!

Having by a miracle made straight Kubjá, the humpbacked servant of Kaṁsa, he killed that usurper and restored the rightful monarch, Ugrasena, to the throne. By this revolution Krishṇa made an enemy of Jarásandha, king of Mágadha, the father-in-law of Kaṁsa, who with a mighty host made war against Ugrasena, but Krishṇa defeated him seventeen times. Threatened by Kálayávana, the king of the *Yavanas* and his mlеccha host, as well as by the king of Mágadha, Krishṇa built the city of Dwáraká, 'the city of gates,' in the country of Guzerat near the western sea. In that city he erected magnificent palaces, dug reservoirs for water, made beautiful gardens, and defended the whole with high ramparts. There he transferred Ugrasena and all the inhabitants of Mathurá and Vrindávana. In that celebrated city Krishṇa lived the life of a voluptuary in the company of eight wives and sixteen thousand concubines! Rukminí, the daughter of the king of Vidarbha, was his favourite wife. She was betrothed to his cousin, Sisupála, king of Chedi; but, while attending the nuptial ceremonies Krishṇa fell in love with her, and taking her away by force in his chariot married her. He is said to have had one hundred and eighty thousand children!

When on a visit to Indra Krishṇa abused his hospitality by stealing the párijáta tree, the tree of paradise, which was produced by the churning of the ocean. The result was a great war between the gods and Krishṇa, in which Krishṇa was victorious. He also fought with the King of Benares and destroyed both the king and the city. At last he exterminated his own race, the Yadus, and soon after a stray shot in the foot from a hunter put an end to his earthly life.

Such was Krishṇa according to the Mahábhárata, the Puráṇas, and Harivaṁsa. He was an extraordinary mixture of contradictory characteristics, for he was a disciple, a devotee, a philosopher, a warrior, a thief, a liar, a murderer and a debauchee! It was the fusion of Vishṇu with this popular hero that contributed mostly to the formation and success of the religion of Vishṇu. Krishṇa was probably a deified hero of great renown worshipped as a *Kuladeva* long before his absorption into Vishṇuism. His name is first mentioned in the Chándogya Upanishad as Krishṇa, the son of Devakí, and pupil of the sage Ghora who taught him the *purusha-sacrifice.* In many passages of the Mahábhárata he is represented as doing homage to Mahádeva (Siva) and receiving from him boons of various kinds, especially weapons of war. He advised Arjuna to apply to Siva for the loan of the weapon *Pásupata* to slay Jayadratha ; and both he and Arjuna worshipped that god. Indeed he is said to have performed austerities for a thousand years to propitiate Siva and received in return wives and children. He even recommended Arjuna to worship Durgá, the fierce wife of Siva. He is, however, often represented as identical with Vishṇu. Hence he justifies the homage he paid to Siva by declaring that Siva is one essence with Vishṇu or with himself. He says to Arjuna, "Rudra, (Siva) with braided hair and matted locks, the frequenter of cemeteries, the performer of awful rites, the devotee, the very terrible, he who swept away Daksha's sacrifice and put out Bhaga's eyes, is to be understood by thee to possess in every age the nature of Náráyaṇa. For when that god of gods, Mahádeva, is worshipped, the god Náráyaṇa is also worshipped. I am the soul of all the worlds. It was therefore myself whom I formerly worshipped as Rudra. If I were not to worship Ísána, the boon-bestowing Siva, no one would worship myself. An authoritative example is set by me which the world follows. Authoritative examples are to be reverenced; hence I reverence Siva. He who knows him knows me; he who loves him loves me. Rudra and Náráyaṇa one essence, divided into two, operate in the world in a manifest form in all acts. Reflecting in my mind that no boon could be conferred upon me by any one, I yet adored the ancient Rudra, the lord, that is, I with myself adored myself. For Vishṇu does not do homage to any god, except himself; hence I in this sense worship Rudra." *

---

* कपर्दी जटिलो मुण्डः श्मशानगृहसेवकः ।
उग्रव्रतधरो रुद्रो योगी परमदारुणः ॥
दक्षक्रतुहरश्चैव भगनेत्रहरस्तथा ।
नारायणात्मको ज्ञेयः पाण्डवेय युगे युगे ॥
तस्मिन् हि पूज्यमाने वै देवदेवे महेश्वरे ।
संपूजितो भवेत् पार्थ देवो नारायणः प्रभुः ॥
अहमात्मा हि लोकानां विश्वानां पाण्डुनन्दन ।
तस्मादात्मानमेवाग्रे रुद्रं संपूजयाम्यहं ॥
यद्यहं नार्च्चयेयम्वै ईशानां वरदं शिवम् ।
आत्मानं नार्च्चयेत् कश्चिदिति मे भावितात्मनः ॥
मया प्रमाणं हि कृतं लोकः समनुवर्त्तते ।
प्रमाणानि हि पूज्यानि ततस्तं पूजयाम्यहं ॥
यस्तं वेत्ति स मां वेत्ति योऽनु तं स हि मामनु ।
रुद्रो नारायणश्चैव सत्त्वमेकम् द्विधाकृतम् ॥
लोके चरति कौन्तेय व्यक्तिस्थं सर्वकर्मसु ।
न हि मे केनचिद्देयो वरः पाण्डवनन्दन ॥
इति संचिन्त्य मनसा पुराणं रुद्रमीश्वरम् ।
पुत्रार्थमाराधितवानहमात्मानमात्मना ॥
नहि विष्णुः प्रणमति कस्मै चिद्विबुधाय च ।
ऋतंआत्मानमेवेति ततो रुद्रं भजाम्यहम् ॥

**Mahábhárata, Sántiparva, 341, 13-26.**

No doubt the votaries of Siva tried their best to absorb Krishṇa into their cult, and they nearly succeeded, for Krishṇa relates to Yudhishṭhira the happiness and glory which he had acquired by adoring Siva, and exclaims, "There is nothing O king, which subsists, superior to Mahádeva, for he is the most excellent of beings in the three worlds. Neither Gods, nor Asuras (demons), nor Gandharvas (demi-gods) nor any one whom the holder of the bow looks upon with terrific aspect, can enjoy tranquillity." He then proceeds to declare that Mahádeva is identical with all existing things. But the votaries of Vishṇu triumphed, and incorporated him with Vishṇu. Not without opposition, however, for Sisupála, king of Chedi, Duryodhana, son of Dhritaráshṭra, Karṇa, and Salya, king of Madura and others strenuously opposed his elevation into a god.

The immoral character of Krishṇa as a god did not elude the observation of the wise in old times. We read in the Bhágavata-puráṇa that a certain king said, "The divine lord of the world became partially incarnate for the establishment of virtue and the repression of its opposite. How did he, the expounder, author and guardian of the bulwark of righteousness, practise its contrary, the corruption of other men's wives? With what object did the lord of the Yadus (Krishṇa) perpetrate that which was blameable?" The answer given is characteristic alike of the subtlety and immorality of the Hindu mind. "The transgression of virtue, and the daring acts which are witnessed in superior beings, must not be charged as faults to those glorious persons, as no blame is imputed to fire, which consumes fuel of every description. Let no other than a superior being ever even in thought practise the same ; any one, who through folly, does so perishes. The word of superior beings is true and should be observed, but not their conduct. They are altogether beyond the sphere of virtue and vice ; and hence are not to be judged after the standards of men. Since Munis (pious sages) are satisfied by worshipping the pollen from the lotus of his feet, and by the force of abstraction have shaken off all the fetters of works,—since even they are uncontrolled, and act as they please, why should there be any restraint upon him, the Supreme Being, when he has voluntarily assumed a body ? He who moves within the Gopís (milk men's wives) and their husbands, and all embodied beings, is their superintendent, who only in sport assumed a body upon earth. Taking a human form out of benevolence to creatures, he practises such sports that those who hear of them may become devoted to himself. The male inhabitants of *Vraja* harboured no ill-will to Krishṇa, since, deluded by his illusion, they each imagined that his own wife was by his side."* The author of the Puráṇa then declares " that

---

* संस्थापनाय धर्मस्य प्रशमायेतरस्य च ।
अवतीर्णो हि भगवानंशेन जगदीश्वरः ॥
सकथं धर्मसेतूनां वक्ता कर्ताभिरक्षिता ।
प्रतीपमाचरद्ब्रह्मन् परदाराभिमर्शनम् ॥
आप्तकामो यदुपतिः कृतवान् वै जुगुप्सितं ।
किमभिप्रायएतन्मे संशयं छिन्धि सुव्रत ॥
धर्मव्यतिक्रमो दृष्ट ईश्वराणाश्च साहसं ।
तेजीयसां न दोषाय वह्नेस्सर्व भुजो यथा ॥

the person who listens with faith to the narratives of Krishṇa's sports with the cowherds' wives, or who repeats them to others, shall attain strong devotion to that deity, and the speedy fulfilment of his heart's desires."

---

नैतत्समाचरेज्जातु मनसापि ह्यनीश्वरः ।
विनश्यत्याचरन् मौढ्याद्यथा रुद्रोऽब्धिजं विषं ॥

ईश्वराणां वचस्सत्यं तथैवाचरितं क्वचित् ।
तेषां यत्स्ववचो युक्तं बुद्धिमांस्तत्तदाचरेत् ॥

कुशला चरितेनैषामिहचार्थो नविद्यते ।
विपर्ययेण चानर्थो निरहङ्कारिणा प्रभो ॥

किमुता खिल सत्त्वानां तिर्यङ्मर्त्य दिवौकसां ।
ईशितु स्श्चेशितव्यानां कुशलाकुशलान्वयः ॥

यत्पादपङ्कज पराग निषेवतृप्ता योगप्रभावविधुताखिलकर्मबन्धाः ।
स्वैरं चरन्ति मुनयोपि ननह्यमानास्तस्येच्छयात्तवपुषः कुतएवबन्धः ॥

गोपीनां तत्पतीनांच सर्वेषांचापि देहिनां ।
योन्तश्चरति सोध्यक्षः एषक्रीडन देहभाक् ॥

अनुग्रहाय भतानां मानुषं देहमाश्रितः ।
भजते तादृशीः क्रीडायाश्श्रुत्वा तत्परोभवेत् ॥

नासूयन् खलु कृष्णाय मोहितास्तस्य मायया ।
मन्यमनास्स्वपार्श्वस्थान् स्वान् स्वान् दारान् व्रजौकसः ॥

Bhág. Puráṇa x. 33, 27—38. Muir's Sanskrit Texts, Part iv., pp. 42-3.

The immoralities of Krishṇa and other gods are defended on the ground that the gods are not subject to restraints like human beings, or that what we consider immoralities in them are only mystic symbols of spiritual realities! This is the kind of sophism used in India to-day by all classes, educated and uneducated, to justify the disgusting acts of the gods.

But Krishṇa has another aspect. The Bhagavad Gítá was written in the interest of Vishṇuism, at a time when the rivalry between the Vishṇu and Siva sects had reached a point of bitter hatred, which (if not already begun) soon broke out into open hostility. The author of the Bhagavad Gítá, desiring to reconcile and unite both parties in a philosophico-religious system with Krishṇa as the Supreme Being, wrote the "Divine Lay," in which the distinguishing characteristics of Krishṇa in the Mahábhárata and Puráṇas are discarded, and the grosser elements of his conduct eliminated. He appears, therefore, as the Supreme Being in human form without the coarse human frailties which the legends ascribe to him. Nevertheless, the author of the Bhagavad Gítá acknowledges that Krishṇa is the inspirer alike of good and evil, and that he sanctions the idolatry, which has always been the bane of India, by declaring to Arjuna that "even those who devoutly worship other gods with the gift of faith worship me." Thus characterizing God as a Being according to every man's ideal! To the philosopher He is the highest generalization of philosophy, the real under the phenomenal; to the worldly He is the bestower of the good things of this life; to the cruel and the sanguinary He is a malignant demon to be propitiated by bloody sacrifices. All these ideals are prevalent in India and, according to Krishṇa, they are only different manifestations of himself; hence those who worship one or all of them worship him, for he is the all!

To make Vishṇu acceptable to the aborigines, the leaders of the Bráhmanical "Reaction" not only fused him with the principal animals worshipped by them, but associated him very closely with others that were worshipped by certain tribes or held in reverence by all,—such as the serpent, the vulture, the monkey and the bear. The serpent has received the homage more or less of all peoples during the past ages. It was the chief god of the Nágas, the non-Aryan people who gave their name to the district and city of Nágpore, and it is revered to-day by all the inhabitants of India. When Vishṇu sits, it is under a canopy of serpents; when he sleeps, it is on a couch made of serpents; and carved images of serpents adorn his temples. The vulture is still worshipped in south India and regarded as the vehicle of Vishṇu. In his Ráma incarnation Vishṇu was intimately connected with the monkey and the bear. Hanuman, the leader of the monkey army, is daily worshipped in the form of every monkey throughout India.

The leaders of the Bráhmanical "Reaction" went further still. They brought Vishṇu into intimate relationship with the Sálagráma and Tulasí fetishes of the aborigines. The Tulasí is variously spoken of as a Gopí in Goloka, the heaven of Krishṇa, as the wife of an Asura and as the wife of Vishṇu. Her body was transformed into the river Gandakí and her hair into the Tulasí plant. After being separated from her for a time Vishṇu was reunited with her in the form of the Sálagráma stone in the holy waters of the Gandakí. In this way the legends connect Vishṇu with the Tulasí plant and the Sálagráma stone. The Tulasí plant was a goddess, an emblem of the Gauda-Dravidian Sakti, and the Sálagráma stone was probably an emblem of her counterpart, Aiyanár, long before the Aryan invasion.

The Sálagráma is a much water-worn concretion, containing ammonites and other shells, found in the river Gandakí within the limits of Nepaul. It is mostly ball-like in shape and perforated in one or more places by worms, or as the Hindus believe, by Vishṇu in the shape of a reptile. According to the number of perforations and spiral curves in each stone, it is supposed to contain Vishṇu in various incarnations. The stones are commonly black in colour, but some are blue, violet, green, yellow, brown, red and white. The Sálagrámas, according to their quality, can produce various effects upon their worshippers. A small one secures heavenly reward, a cool one gives pleasure, a black one fame, a red one sovereignty, a soft one fulfils the desires of the worshippers, one with a wide hole destroys a family, one with crooked curls creates fear, one in which the *cakras* (round marks) are arranged inversely causes misery, a smoke-coloured stone makes one stupid, a brown kills the wife of its owner and one with many holes turns its worshippers into tale-bearers.*

A Sálagráma stone should be worshipped in every house, otherwise such a house is like a burning ground (burying ground). It should not be touched by a Súdra, an outcaste, or a woman. It should be carefully kept in a place apart, wrapt in a clean cloth between Tulasí leaves. It should be washed often and perfumed, and the water used for this purpose becomes holy and is drunk as such. If the Sálagráma be shown to a dying man, and water dripping from the Tulasí plant be sprinkled upon him through its

---

* **Bhàratavarsha, pp. 337-359.**

perforations the effect will be the same as dying in Benares, *viz.*, forgiveness of sin and entrance into Brahma.

Vishṇu as represented in paintings is of a dark blue colour with four arms, holding in his four hands a disc, a shell, a club and a lotus. He wears a crown on his head and a trident-like mark on his forehead. His whole body is covered with pearls, jewels, gold and silver; his garments are embroidered with gold; garlands of flowers and Sálagráma-stones encircle his body; he rests his feet on a lotus flower and rides on a garuḍa—a bird still worshipped at the Poṅgal feast.

The chief Aryan elements in the constitution of Vishṇu are—his name, the pervader; his benevolence; the hero demi-gods—Vámana, Parasuráma, Ráma, Krishṇa and Buddha—in whom he became incarnate.

The chief non-Aryan elements in his constitution are the Gauda-Dravidian animal gods—the fish, the tortoise, the boar and the lion—whose forms he assumed, and probably the doctrine of incarnations. The Sálagráma fetish in which he dwells, the serpent, the monkey, the bear and the Tulasí plant with which he is so closely connected, are also Gauda-Dravidian.

The benevolence of Vishṇu, the root idea of a sun-god—because it warms, lightens and fructifies—is never lost sight of in any of his incarnations, for every one of them has some good end in view. He says in the person of Krishṇa "Every time that religion is in danger, and iniquity triumphs, I come forth. For the defence of the good and the suppression of the wicked, for the establishment of Justice, I manifest myself from age to age."*

By means of the doctrine of incarnations the promoters

* Bhagavad Gítá, IV. 6, 7.

of the Bráhmanical "Reaction" brought Vishṇu from the abstract to the concrete, from the distant sky to the human heroes of the Aryans, and the animal gods of the aborigines. And in this they manifested profound wisdom. They realized that none but a personal God, capable of feeling and sympathizing with suffering humanity, could counteract the influence of Buddhism which breathed so much love and tenderness. It is a thousand pities, however, that in the evolution of Vishṇu the moral side of his character was allowed to deteriorate until in Krishṇa, his most renowned incarnation, it reached the lowest depth of degradation!

4.—*Siva.*

There is every probability that the cult of Siva is older than that of Vishṇu, for the Mahábhárata, which in its present form is conceived in the interests of Vishṇu, presupposes the worship of Siva. Krishṇa and Arjuna worshipped him; the Kings of Mágadha and Sindhu were his votaries; he had his shrine in Gokarṇa on the west and in Kaliṅga on the east coast; he was worshipped in the form of the liṅga in the south and in Ceylon by Rávaṇa and his Rákshasas. Prof. Lassen thinks that he was the god of the Kurus; and he is generally supposed to be the Dionysius of Megasthenes who was worshipped on the mountains, 300 B. C. "The first Hindu representations of a character unmistakeably religious found on coins of the Indo-Scythian Kings about the beginning of the Christian era are Saivite figures alternating with Buddhist symbols. The most ancient dramatic literature, as well as works of romance, is under Saivite patronage. To Siva is ascribed the origin of Grammar, and his son, Gaṇésa, is the patron of letters and arts."*

* Barth's Religions of India, pp. 196-7.

Siva is not a god in the Vedas. He is a later creation, the result of the *blending* of the Vedic Rudra with non-Aryan deities, and more especially with the liṇga fetish. Rudra, the howler or roarer, the father of the Maruts, storm gods, is a prominent god in the Vedas. He is described as wise, bountiful and the strongest and most glorious of beings; as the lord (*Ísána*) of this world; mighty, exalted and undecaying; as knowing the doings of men and gods; as self-dependent and deriving his renown from himself; as the lord of heroes, songs and sacrifices; as tawny-coloured, with a beautiful chin; as fair complexioned, multiform, fierce, arrayed in golden ornaments; youthful, terrible, destructive, wearing braided hair (*Kapardin*); and as the celestial boar. He is identified with Agni (fire). He sits on a chariot, wielding the thunderbolt, and armed with bow and arrows, he discharges his shafts from the sky to the earth. He is represented as benevolent, mild, easily invoked, gracious (*Siva*), and the cause of health and prosperity to man and beast. He is the possessor of healing remedies and is called the greatest of physicians. His twofold nature of fierce and mild we shall see again in the fully developed Siva, the destroyer and preserver.*

---

* "Bráhmans versed in the Veda know two bodies of this god, one awful, one auspicious; and these two bodies again have many forms. The dire and awful body is fire, lightning, the sun. The auspicious and beautiful body is virtue, water, and the moon. The half of his essence is fire, and the moon is called the (other) half. The one, which is his auspicious body, practises chastity: while the other, which is his most dreadful body destroys the world. From his being lord (*ísvara*) and great (*mahat*), he is called Mahésvara. Since he consumes, since he is fiery, fierce, glorious, an eater of flesh, blood, and marrow,—he is called Rudra. As he is the greatest of the gods, as his domain is wide, and as he preserves the vast universe,—he is called Mahádeva. Since he constantly directs all men in all their acts, seeking their welfare (Siva), he is therefore called Siva.—Mahábhárata Anusásana Parva.

In the Vedas there are no definite functions ascribed to Rudra, such as are ascribed to Indra and Agni, or even to Vishṇu. He is called the father of the Maruts, and from this we might expect that he would be represented more eminently than they as the generator of tempests and the chaser away of the clouds. There are, however, but few, if any traces of such agency ascribed to him. The epithets attributed to him are not definite enough to fix the sphere of his operations, or even to define his personality, for they are equally applied to other deities. For example, the epithets "fierce," "tawny coloured," and even "Kapardin" are ascribed to Púshan. But while the cosmical functions of Rudra are vaguely represented, his relation to the good and evil which befall man is clearly expressed. And though he is asked to bestow prosperity, and is invoked as the possessor of healing remedies, he is chiefly regarded as a *malevolent* deity, whose destructive shafts, the source of disease and death, the worshipper strives to avert by prayers. This being so, the remedies which he dispenses may be regarded as nothing more than the cessation of his destroying work; and the consequent restoration to health and prosperity of his votaries.

From this account of Rudra it is not difficult to conceive how a god, "fierce," "terrific," "impure" and "repulsive," such as Siva, could be easily evolved. And as destruction, according to Hindu cosmology, implies recreation and preservation, Siva, the destroyer, would necessarily emerge into Mahádeva, the Supreme Being, performing the functions of creation, destruction and preservation. The epithets by which Siva is pre-eminently distinguished he inherited from Rudra, such as "Nilakantha," the blue-necked, "thousand-eyed," "clad in skins, "dweller in the mountains," "lord of thieves," "the robber," "the deceiver," "the lord of pilferers," "Bhava" the prosperous, "sarva," the archer, and "paśupati," the lord of cattle or of victims. Even the name Siva is an epithet of Rudra raised into a proper name; and the process is visible in the white Yajur-Veda, 3 : 63, where we read "Thou (Rudra) art Siva by name," *i.e.*, thou art gracious by name. Thus the adjective Siva became a noun, another name for Rudra, and hence we read in post-Vedic literature "Rudra is Siva."*

Such is Siva on his Aryan side.† But had Siva remained simply an Aryan god, a Rudra under another name, he could never have become the supreme object of adoration for more than half the inhabitants of India.‡ As in the case of Vishṇu, the Bráhmans had to fuse him with the objects of worship prevalent among the aborigines. It might be objected that, as Vishṇu had already absorbed the gods of the aborigines, there were none left for Siva. It must be remembered, however, that India is a great country; that the Gauḍa-Dravidian aborigines, though belonging to the same race, came to India at different times, lived apart in different localities; and that though they acknowledged all the gods worshipped by the various

* Muir's Sanskrit Texts, Part IV, pp. 341-2.

† Indeed this statement may be too strong for the Satarudriya, the hymn to the hundred Rudras, in the white Yajur-Veda is evidently of a late date, and was probably composed with the view of popularising Rudra, and hence contains some non-Aryan elements. It is altogether in style and structure non-Vedic.

‡ "Siva can reckon up more sanctuaries than any other god. From one end of India to the other at every step, we meet with his temples and chapels, sometimes mere niches or mounds of earth, where he is worshipped principally under the form of the Linga."

tribes—as Hindus do to-day in spite of sectarian bigotry—yet, there were *Kuladévas*, or tribal gods, to whom they paid preferential homage. Whilst Vishnu, therefore, absorbed many of these, the *demons*, the *linga-fetish*, and *certain animals* were left to be absorbed by Siva.

(1) The Vedic Aryans acknowledged and feared devils but did not worship them. They invoked Indra and the other gods to destory them; and there are many formulas in the Atharva-Veda to be used as charms to ward off their attacks.

Demonolatry is peculiar to the Turanian races. Among them it has existed from prehistoric time, and is still flourishing throughout Northern, Central and Southern Asia; in Siberia, Kamtchatka, Tartary and Mongolia up to the confines of China; in the whole of India, especially in the districts of Nágpore, Guzerat, Kanara, Malabar, Tinnevelly and Travancore.

The common names for devils in South India are *Bhútas, Pisáchas, Péys*, the latter being their name in Tamil. Some Hindus are of opinion that they were originally good, but in consequence of sin lost that state, and becoming devils were sent into the world to torment evil doers. Their number is legion and it is constantly increasing, for all who die suddenly or meet with a violent death, either at their own hands or otherwise, are added to them. Besides, men's evil passions, which lead to temptation and perdition, are personified and added to their community. In appearance they are dark, emaciated and frightful; indeed they are so ugly that they themselves are terrified at their own hideousness and run away at the sight of their own images! They dwell on mountain peaks, in deserts, in malarious marshes, in the ocean, in trees, such as the Palmyra, Umbrella and Tamarind. Some haunt houses or hover about in the air, some wander restlessly from place to place, and others make their abode in burial and burning grounds and places of execution. They are always hungry and thirsty. And though their throats are as small as the eye of a needle they can swallow at one gulp twelve buckets of water, and eat voraciously all sorts of food, not rejecting even dirt and refuse!

Hindu men and women, especially the latter, are supposed to be occasionally possessed with devils. The possessed writhes, cries, shouts, runs and performs all manner of mad antics with the firm belief that a devil has seized him. An exorcist is immediately called, who by means of incantations and ceremonies—the most effectual of which is to beat the devil by beating the possessed—casts out the evil spirit and releases the patient. A sumptuous feast, consisting of animal flesh and spirituous liquors, is then given in honour of the event.*

The chief of the devils is Aya, Ayya or Aiya, the ancient Gauḍa-Dravidian word for father, lord and master. † In Tamil he is called honorifically *Aiyanár*, in the plural, and in Kanarese *Ayyappa*. Aiyanár, the father, and his counterpart *Amma*, the mother, represent the mystery of generation and reproduction which forms the centre of Gauḍa-Dravidian mythology. From this centre radiate the cults of the *linga* and *yôni*, which are the foundation of Sivasim. Aiyánar once embodied the purest Gauḍa-Dravidian traditions of the true God. He was invoked as the

---

* **Bháratavarsha, pp. 559—561.**

† *Geneologie der Malabarischen Gotter* von Bartholomaeus Ziegenbalg, p. 148.

kind father, the helper of the weak and the protector of all from danger. But as the Vedic deities become Asuras in the Bráhmanic creed, and the gods and goddesses of the Edda were transformed into devils and witches, so Aiyanár and his counterpart Amma fell from their high position and became evil spirits! Aiyanár is their chief and leader; still, his original character appears in the tradition that he often uses his influence to prevent evil spirits from hurting mankind. Hence the people invoke him "O Lord of Ghosts, who is always pleased, who is filled with kindness towards all creatures, protect, protect, O long armed; to thee, O, Sásta, (ruler) be salutation and salutation." *

Aiyanár, when not riding, is represented in a sitting posture as a red-skinned man with a crown on his head, the three common marks of Siva on his forehead, and strings of pearls hanging from his ears and neck. Ornaments cover his arms, hands, feet and waist. He carries a sceptre in his right hand as an emblem of his royal dignity. The upper part of his body is naked; a gay coloured garment surrounds his lower extremities. †

There is scarcely a village in South India without a temple dedicated to Aiyanár. These temples are generally small and stand in lonely places to the west of the village surrounded by lofty trees. "In woods and forests a stone only often indicates the abode of Aiyanár, and from such stones sounds are said to come forth which frighten the neighbourhood. Clay figures of large and small sizes representing horses with riders, elephants and buffaloes, dogs and other animals, are arranged round and under trees as the companions of Aiyanár". At midnight he mounts

* Ziegenbalg, p. 149.

† Bhàratavarsha, pp. 505-6.

a horse or an elephant, and, preceded by heralds and torch bearers and followed by a large retinue, rides furiously sword in hand over hills and dales to drive away obnoxious spirits. Being a great hunter he is called the "Lord-father of hunting." If any should come across him while on a hunting expedition certain death will be the result. No wonder then that the sight of Aiyanár (*Aiyankátchi*) is greatly dreaded.

Aiyanár is the god of boundaries, forests, tanks and rivers. Among his various names are *Maleidéva*, 'mountain god, *Yógi*, 'the ascetic,' *Candáyudha*, 'one who has a fierce weapon,' *Kumára*, 'youthful,' *Sásta*, 'ruler,' *Kshétrapála*, 'protector of fields,' *Villaiyánaiyurti*, 'the rider on a white elephant,' *Arattaikkáppón*, the 'protector of virtue,' *Arya*, 'venerable.'*

Aiyanár is worshipped under different names in different parts of India. By the Bhils and Kolis the most ancient representatives of the Gauḍa-Dravidians, and by the lower classes in the Maraṭha country, he is worshipped as Khaṇdóbá, the Khaṇd or Gond-father, from Khaṇda + bá, the Maraṭhi form of bápá, father. He is also called Khaṇda Rao, the Khaṇd-King. The resemblance between Khaṇdóbá and Aiyanár both in functions and appearance leaves no doubt that they are identical. Like Aiyanár he is the 'mountain god,' rides a horse, and goes forth, sword in hand, accompanied by his wife and a dog to drive away the demons that afflict mankind. Kárttikéya, the well-known Tamil Subramanya, the reputed son of Siva, whose chief work is to lead the army of the pious against their giant foes, assisted by hosts of imps and goblins, is prob-

* Ziegenbalg, p. 152.

ably identical with him. Vírabhadra and Bhairava, or Bhairabo, who are now worshipped as forms of Siva by the Kurumbas, Bhils and other aborigines are also reflections of him. Like Aiyanár, the former is called *Sásta*, 'ruler,' and the latter *Kshétrapála*, 'protector of fields,' and *Bhùtesa*, 'chief of the devils.' There is a legend which seems to throw light on the way in which Vírabhadra was absorbed by Siva. Siva is said to have produced him from his mouth in order to mar the sacrifice of Daksha. Daksha did not invite Siva with the other gods to his sacrifice because he did not acknowledge him as god. Siva felt himself grievously insulted and called forth Vírabhadra to punish him. The device of representing the gods of the aborigines—vultures, monkeys and bears—as taking the part of Vishṇu and fighting on his side in his Ráma incarnation for the purpose of impressing upon the masses his infinite superiority over their own gods, we see in the Rámáyana. And this is probably a parallel case. Siva was a new god and Daksha, the sage, declined to acknowledge him. But his Bráhman promoters were equal to the occasion. They made Vírabhadra, another edition of Aiyanár, to rush forth at the command of Siva and punish his detractor by making his sacrifice of non-effect.*

Siva became heir to all these gods of the aborigines. He absorbed the names and functions of Aiyanár; and the gods who were reflections of him became various 'forms,' or manifestations, of Siva. Aiyanár is known as *Maleidéva*, *Malhara* the 'mountain-god,' and so Siva became *Girísa*, *Himavat*, the mountain-god; Aiyanár is

* Ziegenbalg, p. 165, Wilson's Vishṇu Puráṇa, Vol. I., Chap. VIII.

the Yógi, and so Siva became the Yógi *par excellence*, "going about naked, his body smeared with ashes and his long hair plaited and gathered up in a knot on the crown of his head." Aiyanár is *Bhùtesa*, *Bhùtaràja*, *Bhùtanátha*, 'Lord of ghosts and chief of evil spirits,' and so is Siva.

In the capacity of Yógi and leader of the infernal hosts, Siva is thus described by Daksha in the Bhágavata Puráṇa.* "He roams about in dreadful cemeteries, attended by hosts of ghosts and spirits, like a madman, naked, with dishevelled hair, laughing, weeping, smeared (lit. bathed) with the ashes of funeral piles, wearing a garland of dead men's (skulls), and ornaments of human bones, pretending to be Siva (auspicious) but in reality Asiva (inauspicious), insane, beloved by the insane, the lord of Bhútas, devils, whose nature is essentially darkness. To this wicked-hearted lord of the infuriate, whose purity has perished, I have, alas! given my virtuous daughter at the instigation of Brahmà." This is the description of an enemy,

---

* प्रेतावासेषु घोरेषु प्रेतैर्भूतगणैर्वृतः ।
अटत्युन्मत्त वन्नग्नो व्युप्तकेशो हसन्रुदन् ॥

चिता भस्मकृतस्नानः प्रेत स्रन्ङस्थि भूषणः ।
शिवापदेशो ह्यशिवो मत्तो मत्तजनप्रियः ॥

पतिः प्रमथभूतानां तमो मात्रात्मकात्मना ।
तस्मादुन्मादनाथाय नष्टशौचाय दुर्हृदे ॥
दत्ता बत मया साध्वी चोदनात्परमेष्ठिनः ॥

IV., 2, 13, 6.

which is bad enough; but the following by a female devotee is infinitely worse* :—' He assumes many forms of gods

* ब्रह्माविष्णुसुरेन्द्राणां रुद्रादित्याश्विनामपि-
विश्वेषामपि देवानां वपुर्धारयतेभवः ।
नराणांचैव नारीणां तथाप्रेत पिशाचयोः-
किरातशबराणांश्च जलजानामनेकशः ॥
सर्वलेाकान्तरात्माच सर्वगः सर्वविद्यपि-
सर्वत्रभगवान्ज्ञेयः हृदिस्थः सर्वदेहिनां ॥
चक्री शूली गदापाणि र्मुसली खड्गपट्टिशी ॥
भूधरो नागमौञ्जी च नागकुण्डलकुण्डली ।
नागयज्ञोपवीती च नागचर्मोत्तरच्छदः ॥
हसते गायते चैव नृत्यते च मनोहरम् ।
वादयत्यपि वाद्यानि विचित्राणि गणैर्युतः ॥
वल्गते जृम्भते चैव रुदते रोदयत्यपि ।
उन्मत्तो मत्तरूपश्च भाषते चापि सुस्वरः ॥
अतीव हससे रौद्रस्त्रासयन्नयनै र्ज्वलन् ।
जागर्त्ति चैव स्वपिति जृम्भते च यथासुखम् ॥
वेदिमध्ये तथायूपे गोष्ठमध्ये हुताशने ।
दृश्यतेऽदृश्यते चापि बालो वृद्धो युवातथा ॥
क्रीडते ऋषिकन्याभि र्ऋषिपत्नीभिरेवच
ऊर्द्ध्वकेशो महाकेशो नग्नो विकृतलोचनः ॥

Mahàbhàrata Anucàsana Parva, 14, 136, 137, 138; 150-157.

(as Brahmá, Vishṇu, Indra, Rudra), and of men, of goblins, demons, barbarians, tame and wild beasts, birds, reptiles, fishes, with many varieties of human disguises. He is the soul of all the worlds, all-pervading, residing in the heart of all creatures, knowing all desires. He carries a discus, a trident, a club, a sword, an axe. He has a girdle of serpents, earrings of serpents, a sacrificial cord of serpents, and an outer garment of serpent's skins. He laughs, sings, dances charmingly, and plays various musical instruments. He leaps, gapes, weeps, makes others weep; speaks like a madman or a drunkard, as well as in sweet tones. He laughs terrifically. He is both visible and invisible, on the altar, in the sacrificial post, in the fire, a boy, an old man, a youth. He dallies with the daughters and the wives of the Rishis, with erect hair, obscene appearance, naked, with excited look.†

There is a legend in which Aiyanár is said to be the son of Siva by Vishṇu who assumed the female form, Móhiní, for the purpose of inflaming the passions of Siva. Hence he is called *Hariharaputra*, the son of Hari, Vishṇu, and of Hara, Siva. This seems to indicate an attempt in more recent times to unite the Siva and Vishṇu cults in one like husband and wife. The united forms of Harihara, or Vishṇu and Siva, appear frequently in South Indian sculptures after the thirteenth century A. D.

The fusion of the Vedic Rudra with Aiyanár and the demons of the non-Aryan aborigines is the first process in the formation of the god Siva.

(2) The second is the amalgamation of Siva with the *liṅga-fetish* of the aborigines. Siva is imaged in twenty-

† Literally ingenti membro virili praeditus.

five "forms" or "*lilas*," but the liṅga is his true idol, in which he dwells in a manner so mysterious as to transform the symbol into a reality. Hence the worship of the liṅga is the worship of Siva. The liṅga is a conical stone intended to represent the *membrum virile*, or paternal organ. It is placed on the ground in the open-air, or on a pedestal in the house, or in the temple. It is often found in conjunction with the *yóni* which symbolizes the maternal organ. For it should be remembered that the root idea of the religion of Siva is *sex-worship*, or the mystery of generation and reproduction. The *yóni* is a triangular stone, with a depression on the upper surface, into which the liṅga is inserted. The form of the liṅga-stone may be natural or artificial, but the form of the yóni-stone is always artificial. Natural stone-liṅgas are found in various rivers, but those found in the Narmadá and Gaṇḍakí are the most excellent and efficacious. Liṅgas are also made of metals. "Bráhman householders should use liṅgas of rock crystals, Kshatriyas of silver, Vaisyas of bell-metal, Súdras of earth, and Rákshasas of gold." There is nothing indecent or offensive in the appearance of these symbols, and a stranger looking at them would scarcely know what they are intended to portray.

The origin of the liṅga-worship is shrouded in mystery. In the Mahábhárata we simply read that Siva and the liṅga are identical. In the Liṅgapuráṇa it is stated that whilst Brahmá and Vishṇu were wrangling as to which of them was the greatest god, a luminous liṅga suddenly dazzled their eyes. They examined it carefully but could not fathom its mystery. Thereupon Siva appeared and admonished them to be at peace and then vanished.

"Thenceforward," we read, "the worship of the liṅga is established in the world. The pedestal of the liṅga is Mahádeví (Umá) and the liṅga is the visible Mahésvara (Siva)."* The implication here is that Siva convinced Brahmá and Vishṇu that he was the liṅga and that henceforth they revered it as Siva. The object being to connect Siva with the liṅga, and to represent Brahmá and Vishṇu as acknowledging that connection. There is nothing to show how the worship of the liṅga originated.

As to the date of the liṅga-worship we are also in total ignorance. We don't know the date of the portions of the Mahábhárata which mention the liṅga; neither have we any means of knowing the date of those portions in the Rámáyana which present Rávana and the Rákshasas as liṅga-worshippers. The word "liṅga" is not found in the Vedas but in Scriptures of a later date, when the Aryans had begun to fraternise with the aborigines in consequence of Buddha's schism.

There is nothing in the Vedas to indicate that the old Aryans worshipped the liṅga under any name whatever. The question then arises—Was it appropriated from the cult of the non-Aryan aborigines and fused with Siva in the same way as their demonology was fused with him? Or was it introduced into India after the Vedic age from some place outside and absorbed by the rising cult of Siva.

It is well-known that the Greeks worshipped the Phallus, and that, according to Herodotos, it was introduced into Greece from Eypt. India had commercial intercourse with the West for many centuries before the

* Muir's Sanskrit Texts, Part IV., pp. 328-30.

Christian era. It is possible, therefore, that the Phallus or linga-worship was introduced into India from Greece, or even from Egypt.

It is more *probable*, however, that the Aryans found it among the non-Aryan aborigines and grafted it on Siva. There seems to be a reference to it in two passages of the Rig-Veda where the aborigines are ridiculed as those whose god is the *sisna*, (membrum virile) *sisnadevàh.** Sàyana, the great commentator on the Vedas, explains *sisnadévàh* as "those who sport with the *sisna*," *i. e.*, "unchaste or lascivious persons"; and Durga, the commentator on the Nirukta, explains it as denoting "those who are always dallying carnally with prostitutes." But this sense is scarcely probable, for "unchaste," "lascivious," or "dallying with prostitutes," would not necessarily be terms of reproach in the mouth of a Vedic poet; while, though the institution of marriage was recognized and honoured, no great amount of reprobation could have been attached to unchastity.† Besides, in the word *anṛitadèva*, Sàyana takes *dèva* in the usual sense of "god," and

---

* नयातवं इंद्र जूजुवुर्नो न वंदना शविष्ठ वेद्याभिः ।
स शर्धदर्यो विषुणस्य जंतोर्मा शिश्नदेवा अपि गुर्ऋतं नः
नः ॥

R. V. VII. 21, 5.

स वाजं यातापदुष्पदा यन्त्स्वर्षाता परि षदत्सनिष्यन्
अनर्वा यच्छतदुरस्य वेदो घ्नञ्छिश्नदेवाँ अभि वर्पसा
भूत् ॥

R. V. X. 99, 3.

† *Vide* R. V., I. 167; 4; IX. 112, 4; X. 86, 16, 177.

interprets it "he whose gods are false." In the same way he understands *antidévam** as meaning "near the gods.' Max Müller translates the word *Múradéváh*† as "worshippers of mad-gods." Surely consistency and analogy demand that the word *sisnadéváh*‡ be translated as "those whose god is the *sisna*." If we could be sure, therefore, that the word *sisnadéváh* refers to human beings and not to demons, the enemies of the Aryans, and that the Aryan poets reproach them for worshipping the *sisna*, it would be proof positive that the linga-cult was found by the Aryans among the aborigines at a very early time. In any case linga-worship is not Aryan; it is reasonable therefore, until the contrary is proved, to conclude that it is Turanian.

It is objected that *sisna* cannot be understood as equivalent to linga which means a sign, and is therefore emblematic, whereas the *sisna* denotes not an image but the *membrum virile* itself. It should be remembered, however, that the language is the language of abuse, and in abuse there is always exaggeration. The reality therefore might have been substituted for its emblem. Or it is more probable that in those days the aboriginal inhabitants did actually worship the *living male organ* as many do the living *female organ* to-day! Moreover, the symbol and the reality symbolized, or the living linga and its emblem, are spoken of indiscriminately in the following passages from the Mahábhárata:—"And when the linga remains constantly in a state of chastity, and people revere it, that is agreeable to the great god. The worshipper of the

---

* (R. V., I. 187; VII. 104, 14.)

† R. V., VII. 104, 24; X. 87, 2, 14.

‡ Sisnadéváh means tail in Rig-Veda, I. 105-8.

liṅga who shall adore the image, (*Vigraha*) or the liṅga, of the great god, enjoys continually great prosperity."* Again, "We have not heard that the liṅga of any other person is worshipped by the gods: declare, if thou hast heard, what other being's liṅga, except that of Mahésvara, is now worshipped, or has formerly been worshipped by the gods? He whose liṅga Brahmá, and Vishṇu, and thou Indra, with the deities continually worship is therefore the most eminent, since children bear neither the mark of the lotus (Brahmà's) nor of the discus (Vishṇu's) nor of the thunderbolt (Indrá's), but are marked with the male and female organs. Therefore offspring is derived from Mahésvara. All women produced from the nature of dévi, as their cause, are marked with the female organ, and all males are manifestly marked with the liṅga of Hara"† (Siva). Siva is said to be more gratified when

* Annucásana Parva 161, 15-17.

नित्यं च ब्रह्मचर्येण लिङ्गमस्य यदास्थितम् ।
महयन्त्यस्य लोकाश्च प्रियंह्येतन्महात्मनः ॥
विग्रहंपूजयेद्योवै लिंगंवापि महात्मनः ।
लिङ्गपूजयितानित्यं महतीं श्रियमश्नुते ॥
ऋषयश्चापि देवाश्च गन्धर्वाप्सरसस्तथा ।
लिङ्गमेवार्चयन्तिस्म यत्तदूर्ध्वसमास्थितं ॥

† Ibid. 14. 226-30.

हेतुभिर्वाकिमन्यै स्तैरीशः कारणकारणम् ।
नशुश्रुम यदन्यस्य लिङ्गमभ्यर्चितं सुरैः
कस्यान्यस्य सुरैः सर्वैर्लिङ्गं मुक्त्वा महेश्वरम् ।
अर्च्चयतेर्च्चितपूर्ववा ब्रूहि यद्यस्ति ते श्रुतिः ॥

adored in the form of the liṅga than in any other form. The liṅga is the second non-Aryan element in the constitution of Siva.

(3) And there is a third, *viz.*, *Animalism.* Siva, like Vishṇu, has identified himself with some of the animal gods of the aborigines. The serpent occupies a prominent place in his religion. His earrings and necklace are serpents. Serpents coil round the liṅga, and are sculptured on the walls of his temples. His garments are the skins of tigers, lions and antelopes. His vehicle is the bull. As in Egypt, so in India, the bull has been revered as a sacred animal from time immemorial. Carved stone images of the bull, Nandi, are seen in and around all Siva temples, and in front of liṅgas. The bull is even worshipped as an emblem of Siva, for like the liṅga, it symbolizes fecundity. One of the "forms" of Siva is Ganésa, the Tamil Pillaiyár, the elephant-headed god, who next to the liṅga is the most frequently seen in India. He is the son of Siva by Párvatí, and is adored as the god of wis-

---

यस्य ब्रह्मा च विष्णुश्च त्वञ्चापि सह देवतैः ।
अर्च्चयेथाः सदालिङ्गं तस्माच्छ्रेष्टतमोहिसः ॥
न पद्माङ्का नचक्राङ्का न वज्राङ्का यतः प्रजा ।
लिङ्गाङ्का च भगाङ्का च तस्मान्माहेश्वरी प्रजा ॥
देव्याः कारणरूपभावजनिताः सर्वा भगङ्काः
स्त्रियो लिङ्गेनापि हरस्य सर्वपुरुषाः प्रत्यक्षचिह्नीकृताः
योऽन्यत् कारणमीश्वरात् प्रवदते देव्याच यन्नाङ्कितं
त्रैलोक्ये सचराचरे सतुपुमान् बाह्यो भवेद्दुर्मतिः ॥

dom. The chief characteristic of the elephant according to Hindu notions is cunning. The elephant is worshipped to-day by the Kolarians, a purely aboriginal tribe. As Vishṇu has absorbed the lion, so Siva has absorbed the elephant. The vehicle of Ganésa is the mouse, an animal still adored by the Oraons as their totem.

Siva appears in pictures generally white in colour, though as kála, time, he is black. As Ardhanárisa his body is half male and half female, uniting in himself the principles of generation. He has sometimes one head and sometimes five, each decorated with a crown. His five heads represent Brahmá, Vishṇu, Rudra, Mahésvara and Sadásiva, corresponding to the five actions ascribed to him; *viz.*, creation, preservation, destruction, vanishing and grace. As pañcánana, or the five-faced one, he has fifteen eyes, ten arms and hands; two hands are empty. With the four hands on the right he holds a deer, a lance, a tambourine and a sword, respectively; and in those on the left, a battle-axe, a trident, fire and shield. When represented with one face he has generally four hands, two of which are empty; and the other two hold a battle-axe and an antelope, or a trident and a noose. His other emblems are a rosary, a boar's tusk, and a human skull. He has three eyes, the third standing high in the middle of his forehead, represent the three varieties of time,—the past, the present and the future. On his forehead he wears three horizontal white stripes, and a moon's crescent near his central eye. His body is decked with jewels and gold and silver ornaments; he wears a necklace of serpents, and over his shoulders hangs a garland of skulls. His lower parts are covered with a coloured cloth, and a golden girdle encircles his waist; he stands on water lilies.

Such is the evolution of the god Siva; not an evolution from a lower to a higher plane, but the reverse. As Rudra he had his terrific and benevolent aspects, for after the howling storm came the calm sunshine and the growth of corn and fruits which support life. Then he descended into a devil, the chief of evil spirits, even a mad-devil dancer; afterwards he coalesced with the liṅga-fetish representing the aborigines' cult of sex worship, and lastly, he became identified with some of the animal gods of the Gauḍa-Dravidians!

---

## CHAPTER II.

### THE GODDESSES OF HINDUISM.

1.—*The deification of the female sex is Turanian rather than Aryan.*

In the Vedas the goddesses do not occupy important positions; the wives of the gods derive their greatness from association with their husbands. It was the genius of the ancient Aryans to look upon *male* deities *only* as exercising divine functions. They neither admitted goddesses to supreme authority nor allowed to the wives of the gods an equal share in Government. Pallas Athene (Minerva) the daughter, and Herà (Juno) the wife of Zeus, were dependent on the will of the principal gods; and Indrání, Agnáyí and Varuṇaní, the wives of the great Vedic gods, Indra, Agni and Varuṇa, occupy only a secondary position. *Prithivímátá*, the Earth-goddess, is invoked together with *Dyaushpitá*, the Heaven-father, but she is not supreme. *Aditi*, boundlessness, a personification of infinite space, though represented in some passages of the Vedas as identical with all things, is not a dramatic goddess performing the functions of the great male deities.

The genius of the Turanians is the reverse. They regard *female deities* as Supreme, exercising the great functions of God. The ancient Babylonians worshipped Dakina, the goddess of the earth, as reverently as they worshipped Ea, the lord of the deep. Every Babylonian city had its titular goddess who was worshipped as its founder and guardian. The same practice is in vogue among the aboriginal inhabitants of India. From time immemorial they have worshipped the mother earth, representing the Female Energy, as the Supreme Being, and do so still in its substitute the local *grámadévatá*, who is believed to be the founder or creatress of every town and village. Hence *grámadévatás* are found everywhere, "in the hamlets of the low caste, in the abodes of savages and in the villages of peasants; in the tents of the Abhíras, in the stations of hunters, among shepherds in the fields and in the bazaars; among Súdras and cultivators; in towns and villages; in carpenter's shops, on the roads, and in the houses of weavers."*

This non-Aryan cult has been adopted by the Aryans, so that now almost all celebrated places of pilgrimage from the Himálaya mountains in the north to Cape Comorin in the south are under the guardianship of the Female Energy as represented by Deví, Kálí, or Sakti.

2.—*Sakti, the root idea of the goddesses.*

Sakti is the root idea of Hindu goddesses. She is thus described in the Dévíbhágavata. "She is neither man nor woman, nor eunuch at the time of the destruction of

---

* Smṛitipuráṇasamuccaya as quoted in Bhàratavarsha, pp. 458-9.

the world ; at the time of creation, however, a distinction is made, she is perception, prosperity, firmness, fame, remembrance, faith, intelligence, pity, shame, hunger, thirst, covetousness, patience, beauty, tranquillity, sleep, idleness, old age and truth ; knowledge and ignorance ; desire, longing, strength, weakness, serum, marrow, skin, seeing, true and untrue ; breath, articulate speech and the various veins. What is she not, and what is without her ? Among the gods she is force, and energizes all works whether divine or human. She is chilliness in the water, heat in the fire, brightness in the sun, coldness in the moon ; without her living creatures can neither move nor the gods fulfil their duties."* In fine Sakti is that invisible force by which all things come to pass and by which all things are sustained. It is the *Prakṛiti* of the Sánkhya, the *Pradhána* of the Puráṇas, and the *Amma* of the aborigines.

The *grámadévatás*, village goddesses, are innumerable. They differ in appearance, in names and in legendary history according to the idiosyncracies of different people in different localities ; but they are *all essentially one* in root-idea ; they *all* represent the Gauḍa-Dravidian Sakti, Female Energy, as manifested in the fecundity of nature and personified as mother. Hence great stress is laid in the Harivaṁsa on the fact that this Energy, as personified in Deví, dwells on the peaks of mountains, in the Maláya, Vindhya and Kailása ; that is in Southern, Central and Northern India ; and that she is particularly worshipped by the Sabaras, Pulindas and Barbaras, the chief aboriginal tribes of India who have not appreciably come under Bráhmanical influence.

---

* Bhàratavarsha, p. 426.

At first, this Sakti-faith found external expression in rude shapeless stones protruding naturally from the earth, preference being given to such as resembled a human head. Multitudes of such stones, daubed with red ochre, are everywhere worshipped in South India to-day. Special images afterwards came into use in order to distinguish between the various Ammas of different towns and villages; and thus probably originated idol-worship in India.

The Aborigines adore the earth-mother as the most powerful Being on whom all existences depend, and who, therefore, exercises unbounded influence for good and evil on all terrestrial things. To induce her to yield the necessaries of life she must be propitiated by sacrificial offerings, and nothing is deemed too precious to gain her favour. Grain, honey, flowers and fruits, cocks, pigs, goats, buffaloes and human beings form her offerings. Human beings are not now allowed by the British Government to be offered, still a few cases occasionally occur here and there. The idea of immolating human beings survives and manifests itself in various customs; *e.g.*, when a Mantapan, or structure for the abode of a *grámadévatá*, is consecrated, a human skull or its substitute a cocoanut is necessary for the ceremony. The Todas of the Neilgherry Hills acknowledge that they now offer buffaloes to mother-earth instead of men as formerly; and the Khoṇḍs until lately offered human sacrifices to the earth-goddess.

3.—*The principal personifications of Sakti.*

Though the Female Energy is represented by many names, or personified goddesses, there are *nine* specially distinguished in consequence of their popularity and the large area over which their influence is felt. These are *Ellamma*, *Máryamma*, *Aṅkálamma*, *Pidári*, *Bhadrakáli*,

*Durgá*, *Cámuṇḍá*, *Púrṇá*, and *Pushkalá*; the two latter being the wives of Aiyanár. With the exception of Bhadrakálí, Durgá and Cámuṇḍá, who represent the dark or fierce side of the Female Energy, the others are essentially the same in origin and functions.*

*Ellamma*, the mother of all, is the name under which Sakti is worshipped in the Telugu country. She is adored by all classes from the Bráhmans downward. According to the legends she has the body of a low-caste woman with the head of Reṇuká, the wife of the Bráhman sage Jamadagni, the reputed father of Parasuráma, and is therefore both Aryan and Gauḍa-Dravidian. She is portrayed in a sitting posture with red skin and fiery countenance, wearing a crown on her head with serpents hanging over it. She has four hands. In her raised right hand is a drum, around which a serpent is coiled, and in the other a trident; in her uplifted left hand, she carries a noose, and in her bent left hand the skull of a torn off head of a Bráhman. The skull is said to attract all the blood of men and beasts which is shed in the world, and yet is never full! Images of *Ellamma* are carved in stone and made of metals. Besides being the guardian of a town or a village, she is invoked by those who are threatened by poisonous snakes, by fishermen who are unsuccessful and by those who are in danger on the sea.

*Máryamma*, the *grámadévatá* of the Tamil people, is considered the chief Sakti, or Energy, and hence is called Parasakti. She is identical with Párvatí, the wife of Siva, for she is the mother of Bhairava, Párvatí's son. The Vaishṇavas also claim her for she is called the sister of

* Ziegenbalg, p. 42.

Vishṇu and Kṛishṇa. She is represented in a sitting posture adorned in the same manner as *Ellamma*; but as she is somewhat more cruel than that goddess, she is more feared for causing plagues than beloved for averting them. She will, however, if invoked kill devils when oppressing any one. Small-pox and cholera are peculiarly connected with her and therefore whenever these diseases make their appearance sacrifices are offered to her for their removal.

The chief characteristic which distinguishes *Aṅkálamma* from the previous two is that she is pre-eminently invoked to exorcise devils from women supposed to be possessed with them. A woman possessed with a devil bathes at night and, attended by her relatives and an exorcist, goes in her wet clothes to the image of the goddess. Plantain leaves are placed before the shrine, the possessed woman moves her head in all directions, the exorcist beats a drum, mutters a prayer, and asks the devil his name and why he took possession of the woman. Meanwhile, under the influence of *Aṅkálamma*, she touches a knot tied in her hair without her knowledge. The devil in the person of the possessed being severely beaten with twings of the Arka plant (*Calatropis gigantea*), leaves the woman and takes shelter in a tree. She then gets up, and taking a big stone hurls it at the tree, when the exorcist and her relatives run after her, cut the knot from her hair, wind it round an iron nail and fix it on the tree!

*Pidári*, though represented in a sitting posture like the other three, is much more passionate and fiendlike; hence her red-hot face and body, and the crown of burning fire on her head. A little more development of her character and she naturally blossoms into the blood-thirsty Kálí, Cámuṇḍá, or Durgá, for all three are identical. Kálí represents the mother in her dark devilish aspect, the fit counterpart of her husband Siva as the fierce lord of demons. She is the titular goddess of Calcutta, and in consequence of her savage disposition, is regarded as the queen of female demons. Siva is said to have competed with, and surpassed her, in dancing ; and is therefore known in the Tamil country as "péyódádi," he who dances with a devil. Kálí is represented as a woman in a dancing posture with the marks of Siva painted on her forehead, a fiery crown entwined with snakes on her head, and two lion fangs protruding from her mouth. She has ten hands, two of which are clasped together, and two are empty ; of the remaining six, the three on the right side carry respectively a rope, a parrot and a spear ; and the three on the left, a drum surrounded by a snake, fire, and a trident. Being always in a state of intoxication her eyes are red like those of habitual drunkards. Bloody sacrifices are offered to her for she is always thirsting for blood. Until lately animal sacrifices did not satisfy her ; human beings were demanded and freely offered. According to the Kalikápuráṇa, the blood of a tiger pleases her for a hundred years, the blood of a lion, reindeer, or a man for a thousand years, and the blood of three men for one hundred thousand years !

Kálí is the goddess of the Thugs who regard themselves as her most faithful followers while pursuing their nefarious profession.

Cámuṇḍá is only another edition of Kálí resembling her in character and appearance. She differs from her, however, in having only four hands, two of which stretched out carry the weapons of Vishṇu—a conch and a disc—

while the other two are joined. She stands on the head of the giant Mahisásura, whom she killed, for which deed she is celebrated in Mysore.

Durgá has the head of a sheep; otherwise she does not materially differ from Kálí and Cámuṇḍá.

Púrṇá and Pushkalá, the wives of Aiyanár, have yellow complexions, crowns on their heads and flowers in their hands. They sit, the one on the left, and the other on the right, side of their husband in whose duties and honours they share.

The Ammas, of which these nine are considered the chief, though differing in name, appearance and character, and corresponding to the mild and fierce sides of their counterpart, Aiyanár, or Siva, are *one* in *principle.* They all represent *one idea,* viz., the female passive energy of the deity which finds expression in Sakti or Yóni.

The male, or active energy, finds expression in the liṅga, and both combined symbolise the *total* active power of God in creation, preservation and destruction. The substitution of the symbols liṅga-yóni for their prototypes is the Siva-cult, which is wholly the worship of *sex-dualism.*

4.—*The fusion of Sakti with the wives of the Trimurti.*

As the Vedic Rudra, under the name Siva, was fused with the Gauḍa-Dravidian liṅga, so his wife, Párvatí, was fused with the Gauḍa-Dravidian Sakti. Both the name and functions of the great Mother passed over to her. Among the thousand names which she bears are Umá, Ambá and Ambiká. Umá, Ambá and Ambiká are Sanskrit modifications of the Gauḍa-Dravidian Amma. The initial A is often changed into U in the Gauḍa-Dravidian languages. We often find Umma, and Umá with a single M instead of Amma; and in Sanskrit the initial U is changed into A in Ambá, Ambiká. Many derivations of the word Umá have been proposed, but there is not one so satisfactory as that which makes it a modification of the Gauḍa-Dravidian Amma. Both the name and the cult passed over to Párvatí. Párvatí became the great Sakti symbolized by the yóni, the counterpart of Siva symbolized by the liṅga. In the Harivaṁsa she is described in terms similar to those in which Siva is described. She is represented "as always abiding on fierce mountain peaks, in rivers, caves, forests and graves. She is greatly revered by the Pulindas, Sabaras, and Barbaras; resides on the Vindhya mountains, and is fond of spirituous liquors, flesh and bloody offerings. She is sister to Baladéva, the mother of the swarm of ghosts; she stands at the doors of kings, resides in holy waterplaces and at the confluence of rivers. She is the full moon, the righteous intellect of the sages, and makes the minds of the gods her abode. She is, on account of her deeds, praised by the goblins as the goddess of liquor; she is the Brahmavidyá, (the knowledge of Brahma) among different kinds of knowledge; the whole world is encompassed by her, the movable and the immovable. In her confides the heart, in her rests the mind; she protects from all sins, she should be propitiated." * Indeed in the spirit of the Turanian nations she is glorified as the Supreme Being; and even the Gáyatri, the most sacred prayer of the Bráhmans, has been modified so as to address her in its terms.

Professor H. H. Wilson says, "Those who adopt her

---

* Harivaṁsa, quoted in Bháratavarsha, pp. 431-2.

(Sakti) as their special divinity employ the language invariably addressed towards the preferential object of worship in every sect, and contemplate her as comprising all existences in her essence. Thus she is not only declared to be one with the male deity, of whose energy some one of her manifestations is the type, as Deví with Siva, and Lakshmí with Vishṇu, but it is said, she is equally in all things and that all things are in her, and that besides her there is nothing."*

The Sakti cult has influenced the whole Hindu Pantheon. The old river goddess Sarasvatí † has become the Sakti of Brahmá. She is the goddess of speech, the inventress of the Sanskrit language, and the patroness of literature and music. A feast in her honour is celebrated once a year, when ink-stands, pens, paper and books are collected, cleaned and placed on a platform before her image, and after the performance of certain ceremonies, she is invoked to bless them. When a man has lied, or given false evidence, his sin is expiated by offering oblations to Sarasvatí. Manu says, "In some cases a man who, though knowing the facts to be different, gives such false evidence they call it the speech of the gods. Whenever the death of a Súdra, of a Vaisya, of a Kshatriya, or of a Bráhman would be caused by a declaration of the truth, a falsehood may be spoken, for such is preferable to the truth. Such witnesses must offer to Sarasvatí oblations of boiled rice which are sacred to the goddess of speech; thus performing the best penance in order to expiate the guilt of that falsehood." No wonder that falsehood is lightly thought of in India!

---

* Religion of the Hindus, Vol. I., p. 247.

† Ziegenbalg, p. 141.

Sarasvatí is represented sometimes with two, and sometimes with four, hands. When four-handed, she holds a víná or a lyre, a lotus, a cup and a scroll, one in each hand; and rides a peacock or a swan.*

Vishṇu has three wives; Bhúmideví, Nílá and Lakshmí. The first is the earth-goddess, the second is the daughter of the king of the Gandharvas, and the third is Lakshmí, his chief Saktí. †

Lakshmí is the goddess of wealth, prosperity, and beauty. According to her functions she ought to be the wife of Kubéra, the god of wealth. There are different accounts of her origin. Some say that she is the daughter of Daksha, and others (the most popular) that she rose from the sea of milk when the gods churned the ocean to obtain the milk of immortality. After they had agitated the sea for a long time "there appeared the great goddess, inhabiting the lotos, supremely beautiful in the first bloom of youth, covered with ornaments, and bearing every auspicious sign. Her head adorned with a crown, her four arms with bracelets, her jet black locks flowing in ringlets, and her body, which resembled burning gold, adorned with ornaments of pearls and holding a lotos in one hand."

She is invoked for wives, children, houses, friends, harvests, wealth, health, and happiness. The following invocation addressed to her by Sakra gives a vivid idea of the influence of Saktism on the religion of Vishṇu.‡

"I bow down to Srí (Lakshmí) the mother of all beings, seated on her lotos-throne, with eyes like full-blown lotoses, reclining on the breast of Vishṇu. Thou art Siddhi (superhuman power); thou art Swadha and Swaha; thou

---

* *Ibid.*, 141. † *Ibid.*, 121.

‡ Wilson's Vishṇu Puráṇa, Vol. I., pp. 148, 149.

art ambrosia (Sudhá), the purifier of the universe; thou art evening, night, and dawn; thou art power, intellect, faith; thou art the goddess of letters (Saraswatí). Thou, beautiful goddess, art knowledge of devotion, great knowledge, mystic knowledge, and spiritual knowledge, which confers eternal liberation. Thou art the science of reasoning, the three Vedas, the arts and sciences; thou art moral and political science. The world is peopled by thee, with pleasing or displeasing forms. Who else than thou, O goddess, is seated on that person of the god of gods, the wielder of the mace, which is made up of sacrifice, and contemplated by holy ascetics? Abandoned by thee, the three worlds were on the brink of ruin: but they have been re-animated by thee. From thy propitious gaze, O mighty goddess, men obtain wives, children, dwellings, friends, harvests, wealth. Health and strength, power, victory, happiness are easy of attainment to those upon whom thou smilest. Thou art the mother of all beings; as the god of gods Hari is their father: and this world, whether animate or inanimate, is pervaded by thee and Vishṇu. O thou who purifiest all things, forsake not our treasures, our granaries, our dwellings, our dependants, our persons, our wives. Abandon not our children, our friends, our lineage, our jewels, O thou who abidest on the bosom of the god of gods. They whom thou desertest are forsaken by truth, by purity and goodness, by every amiable and excellent quality; whilst the base and worthless upon whom thou lookest favourably become immediately endowed with all excellent qualifications, with families, and with power. He on whom thy countenance is turned is honourable, amiable, prosperous, wise, and of exalted birth, a hero of irresistible prowess. But all his merits and his advantages are converted into worthlessness, from whom, beloved of Vishṇu, mother of the world, thou avertest thy face. The tongues of Brahmá are unequal to celebrate thy excellence. Be propitious to me, O goddess, lotos-eyed! and never forsake me more."

*Sex-worship,* though performed under the veil of mystical symbols, must necessarily have a most degrading effect on the human mind. We know how the Phallus worship in Egypt, Greece and Italy, filled the towns and villages with sensual men and abandoned women. And sex-worship has done the same in India. No doubt a few esoteric worshippers view the cult in a mystical light unconnected with sensuality. But to the masses it is the strongest incitement to the grossest immorality. Many Hindus belonging to both Vishṇuism and Sivaism, more especially to the latter, are *Saktis par excellence, i.e.,* they worship the Female Energy as the supreme object of adoration. They are divided into two sects, the *Daksiṇácáras,* or the right hand worshippers, and the *Vámacáras,* or the left hand worshippers. The former represent the purer rite of the ritual, and the latter the grosser and more lascivious. The one is based on the Puráṇas and the other on the Tantras. In the right hand ritual edible rice mixed with milk and sugar is presented as an offering to the symbol of the goddess, but in the left hand bloody sacrifices are the most prominent. The former do not indulge in gross obscenities, but the latter indulge in the coarsest sensuality. The left hand worshippers make a naked woman represent Sakti, and address their adoration to the paternal organ. This ceremony is accompanied by the so-called five Makáras, or the five things beginning with

M. *viz.*, *madiya,* drinking liquor; *mámsa,* eating flesh; *matsya,* eating fish; *mudrá,* mystical intertwining of the fingers; and *maithuna,* sexual intercourse. Such a ceremony is called the "Holy circle," the *púrṇábhishéka* 'the complete consecration,' the essential act or foretaste of salvation, the highest rite of this licentious mysticism. No distinction of caste is observed at these orgies, which goes to prove their *non-Aryan* origin. The whole proceedings terminate with the carnal and indiscriminate copulation of the initiated; each couple representing Bhairava and Bhairaví, forms of Siva and Párvatí, and become for the moment identified with them. Hence male devotees of this cult are called Bhairavas and female devotees Bhairavís.*

The Gurus of the Vishṇu sect established by Vallabàchárya, called Mahárájas, who are worshipped as incarnations of Kṛishṇa, have degraded religion to the same depth of sensuality. They demand from their followers the three-fold surrender of *tan, man, dhan,* body, mind and fortune, and the women regard it as their highest duty and the surest way to eternal bliss to place themselves at the disposal of these hypocritical debauches! †

---

## CHAPTER III.

### THE WORSHIP OF HINDUISM.

1.—*Places of worship.*

We have already incidentally touched upon the worship of Hinduism. We shall now give a general view of the whole.

---

* Barth's Religions of India, pp. 204-5.

† Professor H. H. Wilson's Select Works, Vol. I., pp. 256-8.

In ancient times the Aryanr worshipped the deified elements of nature under the open sky; and the Gauḍa-Dravidians the emblems of their village goddesses and devils under shady trees surrounded with images of snakes, as they do still. Before the rise of the Sectarian religions, however, both Aryans and Gauḍa-Dravidians had begun to erect houses or temples for the gods to dwell in.* There is no mention of images in the ancient portions of the Vedas, but there is in the most recent, especially in the Shadviṁsa Bráhmaṇa. Manu denounces image worshippers as those who should be shunned,† and Patañjali, 200 B.C., mentions the images of Siva, Skaṇda, Visákha and Kásyapa. The Sectarian religions of Vishṇu and Siva, which were occasioned by Buddhism, gave a new impulse to the erection of temples; and in this they were only following the example of the Buddhists who erected dagobas and topes everywhere for the preservation of the relics of Buddha.

For the worship of the grámadévatas, or Aiyanár, a rude stone is fixed sometimes in the open-air in the village, or under a tree; sometimes in a temple built with mud walls and thatched roof, and occasionally in one built with more substantial materials according to the ability of the people. This structure is used, not only for religious purposes, but also for transacting the civil affairs of the village. The temples of Vishṇu and Siva are far more elaborate. They are built with massive hewn stones in the form of a square; and the roof, which is also of hewn stones, rests partly on the walls and partly on stone pillars, commonly huge monoliths. The chief

---

* கோயில், house of the king, or God, is the Tamil name for a Temple.

† III. 152; IV. 214.

idol is placed in the holy of holies (*Garbhagṛiha*) which is a small pyramidal structure inside the temple. Some of these temples are very large containing extensive outer courts and buildings for the accommodation of priests and visitors. The entrance into the temple is under a Gopuram, or high tower, ornamented in relief with figures of Hindu mythology. Some of these figures, especially on the Gopurams of Siva temples, represent gods and goddesses in the shape of naked men and women in exceedingly obscene positions. Similar figures are carved on the pillars which support the roof, on the inside and outside of the walls which enclose the temples, and on the huge cars on which the idols are placed and dragged by thousands of people through the streets on festival days. Men, women and children gaze with delight upon them, but the sight is such as to vex the soul of every righteous man! Two high pillars stand erect in front of the large temples similar to those which stood before the temple of Solomon.

India is full of temples. Every village has one or more. These are supported by revenues derived from lands given by former devotees—kings, chiefs and wealthy men—as well as by the voluntary gifts of the pious who visit them. Until lately, Government managed the revenues, paid the priests, and kept the temples in repair. Now the revenues are handed over to trustees appointed by the people, but they manage things so unsatisfactorily that the people are continually petitioning Government to resume the control.

2.—*Priests.*

The priests who officiate in the large temples are Bráhmans, but there seems to have been a time when they fought shy of Siva temples, for there is a Tamil proverb which says "*Siva sothu kulanâsam,*"* 'the property of Siva is the ruin of a family.' The reason is obvious. The Siva religion is chiefly composed of non-Aryan cults. Bráhmans, however, have overcome all scruples and are now found officiating not only in the large temples of Vishṇu and Siva but often in the temples of the gráma-dévatás of the aboriginal inhabitants. Low caste priests officiate also in the small, and occasionally in the large, temples. The low caste Vellálars and Pariahs seem to have some proprietary right in the most celebrated shrines. Indeed in South India many curious vestiges of the ancient power of the low caste still survive in the shape of certain privileges which are jealously cherished, the origin of which is unknown and misunderstood. "These privileges are remarkable instances of survivals from an extinct order of society—shadows of long departed supremacy bearing witness to a period when the present haughty high caste races were suppliants before the ancestors of the now degraded classes whose touch is pollution. At Mélkòta, the chief seat of the followers of Rámánujácharya, the Holeyars, or Pariahs, have the right of entering the temples on three days in the year specially set apart for them. At the bull games at Dindigul in the Madura District which have some resemblance to Spanish bull-fights, and are very solemn celebrations, the Kallar, or robber caste, only can officiate as priests and consult the presiding deity. On this occasion they hold quite a Saturnalia of lordship and arrogance over the Bráhmans. In the great festival of Siva at Tiruvalur in Tanjore, the headman of the

---

* சிவசொத்துக் குலநாசம்.

pariahs is mounted on the elephant with the god and carries his *chauri* (umbrella).

In Madras at the annual festival of Egáttál, the only mother, the goddess of Black Town, when a *tali* (answering to our wedding ring) is tied round the neck of the idol *in the name of the entire community*, a pariah is chosen to represent the bridegroom. In Madras too the mercantile caste, and in Vizagapatam the Bráhmans, had to go through the form of asking the consent of the lowest caste to their marriages, and the custom has not yet died out entirely."*

Pariahs are closely connected with the celebrated temple of Jagannátha at Purí. It was through a low caste man named Básu that the image was found in the wilderness. When Indradyumna, the proud king of Malwa, had sent Bráhmans to all parts in search of it, one came to the wilderness where Básu dwelt. The haughty Bráhman fraternized with the low caste pariah and married his daughter. Básu in the course of time led him blind-folded to the spot where the image of Jagannátha was lying concealed. The Bráhman worshipped the image with great joy and communicated his discovery to the king. Thereupon the king built a temple for it at Purí, and by the aid of Básu, removed the image to that celebrated shrine. And as a relic of the connection of pariahs with that temple it is said that the presence of Jagannátha destroys all distinctions of caste and creed, and hence until lately pilgrims of all castes and no-caste eat freely together during the festival of the god. Even now food prepared and sanctified at Purí is eaten by Bráhmans everywhere without the least pollution.

---

* Mr. J. Walhouse in the Indian Antiquary, Vol. III., p. 191.

The pariahs take their part in pulling the ropes of the cars of the gods in all places where there are celebrated temples, such as Kánchipuram, Kumbakonam, and Srivalliputtur. It is enacted that on such occasions the touch of pariahs does not pollute.*

3.—*Private and Public Worship.*

The Hindus worship the gods in their houses and in their temples; *i.e.*, they have both private and public worship. Their worship is called *Pújá.* The private *pújá* of a Vishṇu Bráhman differs but little from that of a Siva Bráhman. The Vishṇu Bráhman bathes in the morning in a river, or a tank, and paints on his forehead, breast and arms, the distinguishing mark of Vishṇu. This is a kind of triangle made by drawing two perpendicular white lines from the root of the hair to the commencement of each eye-brow, and uniting them by a transverse line. A red perpendicular line bisects the triangle. Then he meditates the Gáyatri, the most sacred prayer of the Bráhmans, facing the sun. Proceeding to his house, the Bráhman spreads a mat on the floor and places the instruments of worship upon it. These are a *lota* or brass vessel containing sacred water, a lamp made like a statue of one of the gods, a cup for oil, a quantity of sacred flowers, a sprig of the *tulasi* plant, and offerings of grain, arecanut and betel leaf. The Sálagráma stone is of course in evidence, for he worships Vishṇu through this emblem. Tinkling the small bell which he holds in his left hand, he places the Sálagráma stone on a small stand which is called *Singhásana,* a throne. He sprinkles it with water, lights the lamp before it, adorns it with flowers, perfumes it with incense, and offers the repast consisting of grain, fruit

* Bháratavarsha, p. 53.

and sweetmeats which he has provided; every act being accompanied with an invocation. In conclusion he walks around the symbol three times, raises his hands in adoration and utters his last prayer, "O Paraméswara! forgive all my sins, I am a poor ignorant man."

After the pújá the Bráhman proceeds to his meal, but is very particular about bathing, cooking and eating. Every repast is cooked by the householder, his wife, or some near relative. It is eaten after washing the hands and the mouth; and should a strange eye happen to glance upon it, it is polluted and cast away. We were very sorry one evening that our eyes glanced unintentionally on the food of a venerable old Bráhman as he sat in the open to eat it. He had been travelling all day in the great heat of the sun, and had arrived at a grove of trees where he was going to shelter for the night. Gathering a few sticks, he cooked his simple meal, and was beginning to eat it when unfortunately we passed him and saw his food. He exclaimed "O Ba!" and threw it away, saying, "I shall have to lie down without eating anything for I am too tired to cook again." The heads of the Vaishṇavas are exceedingly haughty, bigoted and secluded.

Vishṇu Bráhmans are divided into two sects bitterly hostile to each other, called Vadakalai and Tengalai, or the northern and southern sects. The southern claim precedence on the ground that they have among them the Gada, or Guruship of the great teacher Rámánujácharya. To express this division the sectarial marks have been slightly modified. The southern sect make the three perpendicular lines meet between the eye-brows; the northern make the cross line longer and continue the centre line some way down the nose. Similar marks are made on the chest and arms, and sometimes on the whole body. These marks are often stamped upon the persons of youths with a hot iron as a sign of initiation into the sect. Mystically the outer lines on the forehead represent the shell, discus and club of Vishṇu, and the central line Srí or Lakshmí, his wife. The symbol of Vishṇu is regarded as a charm to ward off calamities, to purify from sin, and even to turn away the deadly weapon of *Yama*, the god of death.

The Siva Bráhman after performing his ablutions paints the marks of Siva on his forehead, breast, arms and stomach. These consist of three horizontal lines on his forehead and a round dot in the middle about the size of a shilling. He wears strings of Rudraksha beads on his brow, neck, arms, and waist. He also meditates the Gáyatri and then worships Siva through the liṅga-fetish. A clay liṅga is placed on a dish, or asána, supported by the sacred bull, Nandi, the vehicle of Siva, while a large stone liṅga combining the male and female symbols, stands near at hand. The pújá begins by uttering the prayer Om, *namah siváya*, or 'Om, salutation to Siva.' The bell in his hand is rung to call the attention of the god, the liṅga is anointed with ghee, curds, water and honey, and decorated with flowers. The sacred lamp is presented to it, and offerings of rice, betel and sweetmeats are made, every act is accompanied by an invocation and the whole is concluded by a reverential gesture, and the utterance of the sacred word Om, 'Salutation.'

Public worship in the temples of Vishṇu and Siva is conducted by Bráhmans three times a day, morning, noon and evening. It consists of *Abhishéka*, holy anointing, *Dhúpa*, incense, and *Naivedya*, meat offering, or oblation.

*Abhishéka* is the anointing of the image with a mixture of honey, sugar, cocoanut water and milk. *Dhúpa* is made of odorous wood and frankincense in a censer with which the image is incensed; *Naivedya* is an oblation of various articles of food which are afterwards divided and consumed by the Bráhmans and servants of the temples. This pújá is performed in the innermost part of the temple (*Garbhagriha,*) where one or two lamps are kept burning all night and often all day.

To Aiyanár, the old chief of the devils, sacrifices of swine, goats and cocks, and libations of strong drink are offered by Súdra priests, called Paṇḍárams.*

In Tinnevelly and Travancore dancing forms an important part of devil-worship. The devil dancer is generally the headman of the village, or failing him, any one that the spirit may move. The dancer is dressed in the most fantastic garments of various colours so as to be a worthy representative of the devil whose presence he seeks. The dancing is accompanied by musical instruments, such as tom-toms, horns, clarionets and bells. At first the music plays slowly and the dancer moves slowly; then the music quickens, and the dancer becoming more excited, whirls about, flourishing a staff covered with bells. This continues until he works himself into such a state of frenzy as to lose all control over his movements. At this stage the devil is supposed to take possession of him and the people prostrate themselves before him in adoration! They ask him many questions respecting their welfare and receive answers so vague as to be of no practical use. Devil-dancing is generally done at night.

The Ammas are worshipped by sacrifices similar to

* Ziegenbalg, p. 151.

those offered to Aiyanár, their images being daubed with red ochre, and their necks decked with wreaths of flowers.

Pújá in the temples is accompanied by the indecent evolutions and lewd singing of the dancing girls. These girls are the recognised prostitutes of India. Some of them are dedicated by their parents from their childhood to the service of the gods as the most precious thank-offerings for supposed blessings received, and others are the children of those unfortunate women. The dancing girls are the most accomplished women among the Hindus. They read, write, sing, play as well as dance. Hence one of the great objections urged at first against the education of girls was, "we don't want our daughters to become dancing girls." The dancing girls are partly supported by temple revenues, for they are as indispensable to Hindu worship as the priests. They are from all castes and as *Dásas*, slaves or spouses of the gods, are above caste and may be open to the embraces of all castes. They are also in requisitions at marriages, festivals and social entertainments of all sorts. It is gratifying to see some educated Hindus now agitating against their presence at domestic functions. May they continue to do so until the presence of the dancing girls in the house be regarded as a disgrace by all the inhabitants of India!

The Barbers, who are a caste in India, are closely connected with the religious and social life of the people. They are the musicians of India. They form the village band and play in the temples during the daily pújá. They play also at religious processions, festivals, marriages and funerals.

4.—*Festivals.*

The Hindus observe many religious festivals, and spend

much more time upon them than Christians do on the observance of the Sabbath. They have festivals on the new and full moon and at the time of the eclipses. They have a festival on the new year, the *Pongal*, when the sun enters Capricorn about the 12th of January. It lasts three days; sometimes longer. On the first day the *Bhóga-Pongal*, pongal of rejoicing, is held when relatives and friends invite each other to entertainments and spend the time in mirth and hilarity. On the second day the *Perum Pongal*, great pongal, takes place in honour of the sun. Married women, after purifying themselves by plunging into water with their clothes on, set about boiling rice with milk and sugar, and when they see it bubbling up, they cry, "*Pongal,*" O "*Pongal,*" meaning it is boiling. A portion of the boiled rice, together with fruits, is offered to the sun, invoking him for the general welfare of the people and the production of abundance. On the third day the *Máttu Pongal*, or the *Cow Pongal*, is held. Early in the morning cultivators sprinkle water on the corn sown in their fields, crying aloud "*Pongal,*" "*Pongal,*" meaning "let it grow in plenty by the grace of the sun which has begun its northern course" (*Uttarâyana*). At noon rice and milk are boiled and presented to Indra, praying him to bestow abundant rain, that grass may grow and cattle multiply. In the afternoon cows and bulls are washed, their horns painted with various colours, and dressed with trappings of leaves, flowers and cocoanuts, are brought in herds attended by music to the public place of the village, where the cow-keepers sprinkle saffron, water and mango-leaves upon them, crying "*Pongal,*" "*Pongal.*" The people then with joined hands walk several times round the cattle and prostrate themselves before them four times. Afterwards the cow-keepers and their herds return to their homes.

The *Durgá-Pújá*, or *Dasara*, the *Dépavalee* and the *Ayuda-Pújá* are festivals of great importance. The first is in honour of Párvatí, the wife of Siva as Amma or Sakti under the name of Durgá; the second is in her honour as Kálí; and the third is in honour of the tools and instruments with which the people earn their daily food.

At the *Ayuda-Pújá*, which is celebrated in September, every artisan, every labourer, in short all Hindus make offerings and supplications to the tools and implements which they use in the exercise of their various trades and professions. The labourer brings his plough, hoe, and other implements and offers them a sacrifice consisting of incense, flowers, fruits and rice, and prostrates himself before them. The mason offers similar adoration to his trowel, rule and other tools. The carpenter is not less pious with regard to his hatchet, saw and plane. The barber collects his razors in a heap, and adores them with similar rites. The writing master makes an offering to the iron pencil, or stylus, with which he writes; likewise the weaver to his loom and the butcher to his cleaver.

The women heap together their baskets, the rice-mill, the wooden cylinder with which they bruise the rice, and the other household implements, and fall down before them after making the offerings already described. The tools are considered as deities for the time being. Indeed they are said to represent Durgá, Lakshmí and Sarasvatí, as goddesses of war, wealth and learning; and hence these goddesses are adored and propitiated through the tools. Few, however, of those who celebrate this festival think of these goddesses when adoring their tools. They regard the tools as veritable deities for the time being! Such is the tendency of the Hindus to deify and worship whatever is useful, or pernicious, whether animate or inanimate.

The annual car festivals are seasons of great rejoicings to all classes. The chief gods of the temples are brought out and placed on large pyramidal cars, decorated with flags and tinsel, and dragged through the streets by thousands of pious worshippers. The people of the town and neighbourhood bring to the gods offerings of money, grain, fruits, flowers and cloths, which the priests gratefully receive and appropriate! Formerly these car festivals were attended with much suffering and cruelty for many of the most fanatical threw themselves under the wheels and were crushed to death! The wheels of the car of Jagannátha at Purí were drenched with human blood years after the English came to India. Indeed English officers were present with their soldiers to protect the liberty of those who desired thus to sacrifice themselves to the idol; but fortunately this barbarous custom has become a thing of the past.

The inhabitants of every village hold a feast in honour of Aíyanár, called in Tamil Aíyan-Tirunál, * 'Aíyanár's holy-day.' This feast has no fixed date; it falls either after the first or the second harvest, and lasts from seven to nine days. The images of Aíyanár and his wives are adorned and carried through the streets both morning and evening. Every inhabitant is bound to contribute according to his means towards the expenses of the feast, and to present to Aíyanár special offerings in the form of cooked rice, fruit, drink and flesh. The feast ends by

---

* Ziegenbalg, p. 151.

praising Aíyanár and his wives for the protection which they have given during the past year, and beseeching them to continue their favour during the ensuing year.

All Hindu festivals now are free from cruelty, except the festival of Máryamma, which is still accompanied by "Fire-treading" and "Hook-swinging." Fire-treading seems to have been first practised by some aboriginal tribes in the worship of Draupadi, the wife of the Páṇḍava-brothers, and then introduced into the cult of Máryamma, or rather identified with Máryamma. After the sacrifice of animals and the offering of fruits to the goddess, the ceremony of walking on burning embers takes place. A round moat 25 feet in diameter and 5 feet deep is dug in the covered ground of the temple, or outside near it. Faggots and logs of wood are cast into it, and burnt till the heat is almost unbearable in the neighbourhood of the ditch. Then those who have vowed to tread on the fire, and who have prepared themselves by fasting and abstention from all carnal desires, walk bare-footed on the red-hot embers in the pit; the spectators, meanwhile, chanting hymns. They walk so quickly and lightly that not very much harm is done, but the custom is cruel and barbarous.

Hook-swinging is performed after the consent of the goddess is obtained. If a lizard is heard chirping at her right side, it is regarded as a sign of her consent, and preparations are at once made to perform the ceremony. All the houses of the place are whitewashed and embellished, the verandah floors are painted with red and white stripes, and festoons of mango and margosa leaves are hung across the road. On the third day before the beginning of the feast, a wooden car richly decorated with banners and plantains, is constructed, and the image of the goddess is taken from the temple and placed upon it. On the third day of the feast the goddess appoints the person who is to have the honour of swinging, who in the south is generally a Maravan. White and red flowers are distributed among the competitors who have been preparing themselves for the honour during the previous fortnight. On the fourteenth night of the feast the goddess appears to the chief man of the Maravas and announces the name of the person chosen by her. On the following day the chosen candidate, after drinking himself drunk, has two iron hooks inserted behind the large muscle of his back. These hooks are attached to a piece of iron which is fastened to a pole fixed in the car, so that when the car is dragged through the streets by the crowd, accompanied by music, the man swings to and fro in the air. During the progress of the car sheep are sacrificed to the goddess and the people prostrate themselves before her. On the return of the car to the starting point, the swinger is released from the hook and honoured by the acclamation of the people. Serious accidents sometimes occur when the swinger is killed, in which case he is worshipped as a deity; at other times he falls to the ground and breaks one or more limbs. Government ought to interfere and put an end to this cruel practice, especially now, because revived interest is manifested in the ceremony.

Pilgrimages to sacred places are very popular in India. Worshipping a certain god who dwells in a celebrated temple, or bathing in one of the large rivers which are held sacred results in the forgiveness of sin and purification of the soul. It is not at all an uncommon occurrence to see a whole village going on a pilgrimage to a distant shrine or sacred stream and the sight is very picturesque. Men, women and children, dressed in clothes of various colours, march with the village band in front, and the name of the god whose temple they hope to reach on their lips. It is calculated that there are always 30,000 pilgrims in Benares, and about 150,000 attend the festival of Jagannátha at Puri every year.

---

## CHAPTER IV.

### THE PHILOSOPHY OF HINDUISM.

#### 1. *Philosophy—A Part of Hindu Religion.*

A Dissertion on Hinduism would be incomplete without a glance, however brief, at its philosophy; for philosophy is as much a part of religion in India as prayers, sacrifices and ritual. Nay, more so, for it is the only part of Hinduism that the cultured and spiritual value and pursue.

The philosophy of modern Hinduism is essentially the same as that contained in the six systems which have been already considered. The doctrines of the old Darsanas have been differently stated, and different aspects emphazised, but there have been no new discoveries. The Hindus are in this respect like the Greeks. They lost the power of original thinking after once casting forth great thoughts.

#### 2. *The Bhagavadgítá—Theism and Monism.*

The Bhagavadgítá, the most popular and highly esteemed philosophical book in India to-day, is an evolute from the Sánkhya-Yóga and Vedánta Systems of Philosophy. As it is intended to reconcile the sects of Vishṇu and Siva it is widely comprehensive and provokingly contradictory. It has a side for Theism, for it represents Kṛishṇa as a personal God, eternal, immortal, almighty, full of glory, the creator of the world and the upholder of all things by his power "like a number of pearls on a string." Viewed in this light its philosophy is *dvitíya*, dual. It has another side for Pantheism, for it represents Kṛishṇa as the only one real existence, all phenomena being nothing but his máyá, illusion. Viewed in this light its philosophy is *advitíya*, non-dual.

3. *Saṅkarácharya—Monism.*

The great Siva champion, Saṅkarácharya, who flourished in the eighth century A. D. emphazised the non-dual side of the philosophy of the Bhagavadgítá and formulated what is called the *Sriddhádvitíya*, the correct non-dual or monism; the fundamental principle of which is the Upanishad maxim *eka eva advitíya*, one without a second, which is Nirguṇa Brahma. This Brahma, associating himself with máyá, produced the appearance of the world and of Saguṇa Ísvara, deity with attributes, represented as the creator, preserver and destroyer. Ísvara is Siva; and the philosophy of the Siva sect is *Sriddhádvitíya*.

4. *Rámánujácharya—Qualified Dualism.*

In the twelfth century A. D., Rámánujácharya formulated the *visishtádvitíya* system, a system midway between the *dvitíya* and *advitíya* of the Bhagavadgítá. This system can be understood best by contrasting it with the *advitíya* of Saṅkarácharya. According to Saṅkarácharya's *advitíya* whatever is, is Brahma and Brahma is absolutely homogeneous, so that all difference and plurality must be illusory. According to Ramánujácharya's *visishtádvitíyas* whatever is, is Brahma, but Brahma contains within itself elements of plurality owing to which it truly manifests itself in a diversified world. The world, with its variety of material forms of existence and individual souls, is not unreal, as Saṅkarácharya affirms, but a real part of Brahma's nature, the body covering the universal self. The Brahma of Saṅkarácharya is in itself impersonal without attributes, but becomes personal when associated with Máyá, so that strictly speaking such a god is himself unreal. Rámánujácharya's Brahma, on the other hand, is essentially a personal god, the all-powerful and wise ruler of a real world. Saṅkarácharya's personal soul is Brahma limited by Máyá; whereas Rámánujácharya's personal soul is a real individual, sprung from Brahma but never outside Brahma. It enjoys a separate personal existence, and will remain a personality for ever. The *summum bonum* according to Saṅkarácharya is the merging of the individual soul in Brahma; but according to Rámánujácharya it is the soul passing from earthly troubles into heaven where it will remain for ever in a state of personal bliss. Rámánujácharya founded a religious sect among the Vaishṇavas called after his name, and its philosophy is *Visishtádvitiya*

5. *Madvácharya—Full Dualism.*

Madvácharya, another Vishṇu reformer, who lived in the thirteenth century A. D., developed the qualified dualism of Rámánujácharya into a full dualism. He taught that God, the Paramátman, is one, and man, the Jivátman, is another; the relation between them being that of independent and dependent. God, Vishṇu, is independent, man is dependent upon him but not identical with him. The felicity of the soul after death does not consist in loss of individuality by absorption into the deity, but in conscious enjoyment of bliss in Vaikuṇṭha, the heaven of Vishṇu.

There is a remarkable feature in this system of Madvácharya which differentiates it from all previous Hindu types of religious thought, and which has made some surmise that it is derived from Christianity. A surmise not at all improbable, for the Church of St. Thomas was well established in Malabar as early as 522 A. D., and Christians were in the North in the seventh century A. D. Madvácharya's system teaches that the soul's salvation is dependent on the grace of Vishṇu which is obtained by the knowledge of the excellence of the god, and not by the knowledge of the distinction between him and the personal soul. We read, " It is declared that the grace of Vishṇu is won only through knowledge of his excellence, and not through the knowledge of non-duality." Madvácharya founded a religious sect among the Vaishṇavas and all his followers accept his *dvitiya* system as their Philosophy.

The Philosophy of Hinduism, then, is three-fold—*advitiya*, *visishṭádvitiya*, and *dvitiya*. The first is the philosophy of the Saivas, and the two last form the philosophy of the Vaishṇavas.

---

## Retrospect.

We have now traced the Evolution of Hinduism from its commencement to its completion, or at any rate to a point where it has stood in a state of unstable equilibrium for the last thirteen hundred years. We have pointed out the chief factors which made it possible and necessary, *viz.*, the Disintegration of Vedism and the Reaction of the

Bráhmans. The disintegration of the ancient creed conditioned it, and the natural desire of the Bráhmans to regain their ascendency, which was overthrown by Buddhism, was the immediate cause of the Reaction. We have traced the formation of Hinduism, the cunningly devised scheme by which the Bráhmans gradually regained their power and ultimately banished Buddhism from India. We have shown how the Vedic Vishṇu and Rudra were fused with the animal gods and fetishes of the aborigines and the heroes of the Aryan race; and how those composite gods captivated the inhabitants of India under the altered conditions brought about by the schism of Buddha. We have considered the goddesses of Hinduism who figure so prominently in the system, and have showed that their root-idea is Turanian. We have given a brief description of the private and public worship of Hinduism; a short sketch of its chief religious Festivals; and a bird's eye-view of its Philosophy. In short we have represented Hinduism from the FOUNDATION to the completion of the EDIFICE.

It will be seen that with the exception of Rámánujáchárya and Madvácharya no efforts were made to reform Hinduism in the direction of rational Theism. Subsequent Reformers have done more in this direction, such as Kabír, Chaitanya, the Sikh Gurus and the founders of the Brahma Samáj; but they worked in a different atmosphere under the influence of a foreign environment and hence do not fall within the limits of this Treatise.